FIRSTS, LASTS
& ONLYS
CRIME

First published in the United Kingdom in 2007 by
Robson Books
10 Southcombe Street
London
W14 0RA

An imprint of Anova Books Company Ltd

ISBN 9781905798049

A CIP catalogue record for this book is available from the British Library.

10 9 8 7 6 5 4 3 2 1

Printed and bound by Cromwell Press, Trowbridge, Wiltshire, England

This book can be ordered direct from the publisher.
Contact the marketing department, but try your bookshop first.

www.anovabooks.com

FIRSTS, LASTS
& ONLYS
CRIME

JEREMY BEADLE
& IAN HARRISON

**ROBSON
BOOKS**

CONTENTS

☆ **Firsts**

First criminal caught by fingerprints 1892
First motorist to be fined for speeding 1896
First driver convicted of drink-driving 1897
First woman to be electrocuted 1899
First police car chase in Britain 1899
First police car 1899
First conviction of British criminal based on fingerprint evidence 1902
First British murder solved by fingerprint 1905
First police motorbike patrol 1905
First celebrity trial of the twentieth century 1906
First ASBO issued 1907
First criminal caught by wireless telegraph
First murder in America solved by fingerprints 1910
First getaway car used in a robbery 1911
First case in British history of a crime passionel 1917
First non-political killer hanged in the Republic of Ireland 1923
First execution by gas chamber 1924
First criminal use of a Thompson submachine gun 1925
First FBI agent killed on duty 1925
First mobster to conceal a weapon in an instrument case 1925
First aeroplane bombing raid by criminals 1926
First armoured truck hold-up in US 1927
First escape from Strangeways Prison 1927
First photo of a woman dying in electric chair 1928
First ransom kidnapper in the US to be executed 1928
First inmate to escape from Peterhead Prison 1934
First woman to die in the electric chair in Ohio 1938
First successful escape from Dartmoor Prison 1940
First British 'Public Enemy Number One' 1940
First execution by America's only portable electric chair 1940
First execution at which Albert Pierrepoint was Number One executioner 1941
First woman executed in the gas chamber 1941
First British murder conviction based on palmprint evidence 1942
First British defendant convicted of murder without a body 1948
First FBI Most Wanted named 1950
First British murderer hunted with the aid of television 1953
First 'noddy bikes' 1955
First use in England of bare footprints as evidence 1956
First surveillance camera 1957
First white man hanged for murder of black person in Kenya 1960
First murderer caught by Identikit 1961
First skyjacking in America 1961
First murder transmitted on live television 1963
First criminal caught by satellite 1965
First female addition to the FBI's Most Wanted list 1968
First kidnap-and-ransom crime perpetrated in Britain 1969
First use of Photofit 1970
First female African-American police officer killed in the line of duty 1974
First serial sex killers in Ireland start their campaign of terror 1976
First murder of a federal Judge in America 1979
First to die by lethal injection 1982
First American citizen deported for war crimes 1984
First woman executed by lethal injection 1984
First criminal case to be decided by DNA evidence 1986
First conviction secured through DNA evidence 1987
First murder conviction based on DNA evidence 1988
First conviction of computer hacker 1988
First murderer to appear in a televison reconstruction of the murder 1991
First murder to be broadcast on British television 1991
First execution of criminal convicted on DNA evidence 1994
First man convicted for attempting to rape a man 1995
First Briton to be executed in Singapore 1996
First virtual-reality reconstruction of crime scene used in court evidence 1998
First professional footballer to play in a league match wearing an electronic tag 2000
First parent jailed for allowing children to play truant 2002

First posthumous pardon in New York State 2003
First conviction using DNA 'familial searching' 2004
First ASBO (Anti-Social Behaviour Order) issued in the UK 2004
First internet murder 2004
First airline pilot to be jailed under legislation designed to tackle alcohol abuse 2004
First woman to be convicted of using date rape drug rohypnol to stupefy and rob men 2005
First criminal sentenced by telephone 2005
First killing by a Sky Marshal 2005
First person convicted by evidence from a camera fitted to a policeman's hat 2006

❋ Lasts

Last person executed by the sword in England 1536
Last woman boiled alive in England 1547
Last man burned at the stake in Britain 1612
Last victim of the Halifax Gibbet 1650
Last head publicly exhibited on London Bridge 1678
Last person decapitated by the Scottish Maiden 1685
Last royal execution in Britain 1685
Last person convicted in England of being a witch 1721
Last man executed by the axe 1747
Last person executed in Scotland for bestiality 1751
Last English nobleman to suffer a 'felon's death' 1760
Last witch executed in Europe 1775
Last public hanging in the Commonwealth 1778
Last execution at Tyburn 1783
Last victim of the ducking stool in England 1809
Last culprit hanged in Scotland for stealing a sheep 1818
Last official beheadings in England 1820
Last beheadings in Britain 1820
Last person executed for forgery in Scotland 1827
Last person executed for forgery in England 1829
Last person to be punished in the pillory in England 1830
Last man gibbeted in Britain 1832
Last person in Scotland executed for rape 1835
Last person in England imprisoned for denying the existence of God 1842
Last recorded duel between two Englishmen on English soil 1845
Last execution on Guernsey 1854
Last American pirate to be executed by hanging 1860
Last woman executed in Tasmania 1862
Last woman publicly executed in Scotland 1862
Last man in Britain to commit suicide on the morning of his execution 1862
Last woman to be hanged in public at Newgate 1862
Last British convicts arrive in Australia 1868
Last public hanging of a woman in Britain 1868
Last public execution in Scotland 1868
Last person to be publicly hanged in Great Britain 1868
Last public hanging in Canada 1869
Last hanging by William Calcraft in London 1874
Last execution by William Calcraft 1874
Last public execution in the British Isles 1875
Last woman executed by decapitation in Japan 1879
Last woman hanged in New York State 1887
Last triple hanging at Newgate Prison 1896
Last triple execution in Britain 1896
Last Wild West stagecoach robbery pulled by a woman 1899
Last woman hanged in Wales 1907
Last woman executed in Western Australia 1909
Last man to be executed in North Wales 1910
Last US stagecoach robbery 1917
Last person imprisoned for blasphemy in Britain 1921
Last American Great Train Robbery 1923
Last man executed for rape in Australia 1932
Last man in Scotland to be shackled in a prison cell 1934
Last person publicly executed in Kentucky 1936
Last official public hanging in the United States 1937

Last person publicly guillotined in France 1939
Last execution in the Tower of London 1941
Last person sentenced under the British Witchcraft Act 1944
Last execution by firing squad in Great Britain 1944
Last woman hanged in Australia 1951
Last woman executed in Canada 1953
Last hanging in the Irish Republic 1954
Last side-by-side double hanging in Britain 1954
Last woman executed in Britain 1955
Last execution by Albert Pierrepoint 1955
Last man hanged in New Zealand 1957
Last person to be hanged in UK for murder of police officer 1959
Last man hanged at Pentonville Prison 1961
Last prisoner of Alcatraz 1963
Last execution in Scotland 1963
Last men hanged in Britain (for murder) 1964
Last person executed in South Australia 1964
Last execution in Australia 1967
Last guillotining in France 1977
Last execution by firing squad in the US 1996
Last legal hanging in the US 1996

❏ Onlys
Only English queen arrested for being a witch 1417
Only woman known to have been tortured on the rack 1546
Only couple hanged for adultery in America 1643
Only person to be pressed to death in America 1692
Only persons executed under the bizarre Coventry Act 1722
Only prisoner of both the Bastille and the Tower of London 1747
Only peer of the realm to have been hanged for murder 1760
Only American female pirate executed 1789
Only woman hanged at Berrima prison 1843
Only Harvard Professor to be hanged 1850
Only American executed for slave trading 1862
Only murderer hanged wearing a policeman's uniform 1869
Only US President to have personally hanged criminals 1872
Only woman in South Australia to go to the gallows 1873
Only woman hanged in Queensland 1887
Only jail-breaker to become a judge 1890
Only woman hanged for murder in Britain whose father had also been hanged for murder 1890
Only woman judicially hanged in New Zealand 1895
Only woman electrocuted in the 19th century 1899
Only man in twentieth century to be hanged for murdering his own grandson 1900
Only uncle and nephew executed in Britain 1901
Only private detective executed in Britain 1902
Only woman executed at Armley Jail 1903
Only murder known to have been committed by hyoscine 1910
Only New York City policeman executed for murder 1915
Only albino executed for murder in Britain 1919
Only British solicitor executed for murder 1922
Only professional British footballer to be murdered 1923
Only time the rope broke during British hanging in the twentieth century 1924
Only female official witness at a British hanging 1925
Only double execution in Washington's history 1932
Only person prosecuted under the Honours (Prevention of Abuses) Act 1933
Only criminal officially declared Public Enemy Number One by FBI 1934
Only murder case instigated by a shark 1935
Only dwarf executed in Britain in the twentieth century 1937
Only case in which two rattlesnakes were used as murder weapons 1942
Only Test cricketer to have been executed 1955
Only accused in Britain to claim amnesia as a defence against a capital offence 1959
Only person executed in Israel 1962
Only criminal kidnap attempt on British royalty 1974
Only mass-escape from America's death row 1984
Only prosecution for molesting a dolphin 1991
Only Amish man convicted of homicide 1993

☆ FIRST man in England to be legally beheaded

Waltheof, 1st Earl of Northumbria, at St Giles's Hill, near Winchester. Tuesday 31 May 1076

There were earlier beheadings by sword but Waltheof was the first to be so punished under a law introduced by William the Conqueror for the execution of aristocrats – the Normans considered beheading to be an honourable death. Implicated in at least two treasonous plots against William, Waltheof languished in prison for almost a year after his trial as judgment was repeatedly postponed. Eventually, in semi-secrecy, he was hurriedly executed at dawn on St Giles's Hill near Winchester. One of the few witnesses stated that the sword fell during Waltheof's recitation of the Lord's Prayer and that the final 'but deliver us from evil, Amen' was voiced by his severed head.

DID YOU KNOW?

After his execution Waltheof's body was thrown in a ditch but a fortnight later, at his widow's request, Abbot Wulfketel of Crowland retrieved it for more honourable burial in the chapter house of his monastery. After a fire in 1092 the body was taken from the ruined chapter house to a prominent place in the abbey church, and on opening the coffin the corpse was found intact. Not only that, but the head was miraculously rejoined to the trunk with only a fine crimson line showing where it had been cut off. This miracle began to draw pilgrims to the tomb and many cures were recorded occurring at dawn, the time of Waltheof's execution. After Waltheof's execution the sword was replaced by an axe as the instrument of beheading, with one notable exception: the next and last beheading by sword was that of Anne Boleyn in 1536.

☆ FIRST assassination victim

Nizam al-Mulk, Persia. Saturday 16 October 1092

The killing of Nizam al-Mulk was the world's first political murder, carried out on the orders of Hasan ibn-al-Sabbah ('Old Man of the Mountain'). Sabbah's followers offered blind obedience after being indulged for days with hashish, which led to to the group being called Hashashshin ('hashish-eaters'), a name later corrupted to 'assassins'. Born in Tus in Persia (now Iran) the victim, Abu Ali al-Hasan al-Tusi Nizam al-Mulk, was a celebrated scholar and vizier of the Seljuq Empire. He was renowned for systematically founding the Nizamiyyah schools, which were to become the model for universities later established in Europe. Al-Mulk was killed while being carried to his harem, stabbed in the chest by assassin Bu Tahir Arrani, who was disguised as a holy man pretending to bless him. As he carried out the murder Arrani is said to have cried, 'The killing of this devil is the beginning of bliss.'

☆ FIRST person imprisoned in the Tower of London
☆ FIRST person to escape from the Tower of London

Ranulf Flambard, Tower of London. Wednesday 15 August 1100 to Saturday 2 February 1101

Ranulf Flambard, aka Ralf, or Ralph, was born in Bayeux, the son of a parish priest. After emigrating to England he entered the court of William the Conqueror, where he proved to be an astute financier but was disliked by the barons, who nicknamed him 'Flambard' – an insulting term for a mischief-maker. On William's death Ranulf became chaplain and treasurer to the rapacious William II, extorting the people to fund William's vices and extravagances. The scheming prelate also managed to fill his own pockets, eventually managing sixteen abbeys or bishoprics, and in 1099 taking the wealthy post of Bishop of Durham. But William's successor, Henry I, was keen to dissociate himself from the previous brutal regime, and on 15 August 1100, just thirteen days after William's death, Flambard was arrested and became the first ever prisoner in the newly built Tower of London (then comprising only the square keep now known as the White Tower). On the night of 2 February 1101, after serving 171 days, Flambard generously shared wine with his guards from a cask friends had given him. With the guards in a drunken stupor, Flambard used a rope that had been concealed in the wine cask to climb down to ground. His friends, waiting below with horses, took him to the coast and then to Normandy. From there Flambard made peace with Henry who allowed him to return in 1106 – as penance, he completed the magnificent nave of Durham Cathedral.

☆ FIRST recorded hanging at Tyburn

William FitzOsbert, Tyburn, London. 1196

William FitzOsbert, or Osborn, was popularly known as 'Longbeard' and 'defender of the poor against the royal extortioners'. He led a shortlived revolt against the the heavy taxes imposed on wealthy Londoners to raise ransom for King Richard the Lionheart – Richard had been kidnapped on his return from the Crusades and Holy Roman Emperor Henry VI was demanding 150,000 Marks for his release. (Given that Richard spent a mere 160 days of his reign in England, his subjects' grievances were understandable.) FitzOsbert's insurrection was swiftly and brutally quelled; FitzOsbert sought sanctuary in London's church of St Mary-le-Bow but his pursuers set fire to the church to drive him out. After a summary trial his hands were bound behind his back, his feet tied, and he was dragged by horse to Tyburn where he was hanged alongside nine of his followers. After the execution sympathisers stole parts of the gibbet as relics and took the bloodsoaked earth for use as miracle cures.

☆ FIRST nobleman in England to be hanged, drawn and quartered

David III of Wales, Dafydd ap Gruffydd (aka Prince of Gwynedd), Shrewsbury. Saturday 2 October 1283

As well as being the first nobleman in England to be hanged, drawn and quartered, Dafydd was also the last native Prince of Wales. For several years he fought alongside the English King Edward I against his elder brother Llywelyn ap Gruffydd. Eventually he turned against the king and in 1282, on the death of his brother, he styled himself 'Prince of Wales and Lord of Snowdon' and assumed leadership of the Welsh fight against Edward. After Dafydd's inevitable capture, on 22 June 1283, Edward summoned all the English nobles to Shrewsbury for the trial of 'the last survivor of a family of traitors'. Found guilty of treason, Dafydd's execution was specifically devised to be harsher than any previous execution with the intention of totally eliminating further Welsh resistance. The punishment was meted out in four stages: he was dragged to the scaffold as a traitor; he was hanged for murder; because the murders had been committed during the Lord's passion he was disembowelled and his entrails burnt; and finally, for plotting the king's death, his body was quartered – Geoffrey of Shrewsbury was paid 20 shillings to perform the ghastly ritual. Dafydd's body parts were sent to four English cities for display while his head joined that of his brother Llywelyn on top of the Tower of London, where the skulls were still visible many years later. The final insult was that in 1301 Edward invested his own son, Edward II, with the title Prince of Wales.

☆ FIRST person to have his head adorn the ramparts of London Bridge as a warning to other wrongdoers

William Wallace, London Bridge. Monday 23 August 1305

After apparently being betrayed by his own countrymen, William Wallace was captured and, on 22 August 1305, taken to London. Early the next morning he was taken to Westminster Hall where, to fulfil his boast that one day he would wear a crown in Westminster, a laurel crown was mockingly placed on his head. As an outlawed thief the law allowed him no defence: his trial and judgement were mere formalities and the sentence was carried out immediately. He was stripped naked then drawn on a hurdle by two horses to the gallows at 'Smoothfield' (now King Street in Smithfield). En route he was pelted with offal, garbage and dung and struck with whips and cudgels by the bloodthirsty Londoners. Still naked, he mounted the scaffold and was hanged by a halter but let down still alive. Next his genitals were cut off and then a deep gash made in his belly; the executioner then ripped out his intestines, liver and lungs, holding each aloft for the crowd to see before consigning them to the fire before Wallace's eyes. Then the executioner reached into the chest cavity to tear out Wallace's still beating heart; finally, mercifully, his head was cut off and his trunk cut into four pieces. His head was dipped in pitch to delay putrefaction then spiked and placed on London Bridge. His quarters were later displayed at various towns: his right arm at Newcastle upon Tyne; his left arm at Stirling; his right leg at Berwick; and his left leg at Perth. The total cost of the butchery was sixty-one shillings and tenpence.

DID YOU KNOW?

Wallace, the surname of Scotland's greatest patriot, originally meant 'Welshman'.

❏ ONLY English queen arrested for being a witch

Joanna of Navarre, Havering, Essex. September 1417

Henry IV and his second wife, Joan, enjoyed an apparently happy marriage. Joan's stepson Henry (later Henry V) referred to her as his 'dearest mother' and after Henry IV died in 1413 Joan continued to enjoy the new king's favour. Then, in 1419, things changed: the financial demands of the war with France led the king to cast envious eyes on Joan's dower. In August 1419 the goods of her confessor, Father John Randolph, were seized: in fact it is clear that they were Joan's, including as they did 'a woman's night cap, red after the Breton fashion'. Then Randolph sensationally accused the queen of 'an act of witchcraft which would have tended the King harm'. The case never came to trial but she was arrested, her remaining possessions confiscated, and she was kept a virtual prisoner until July 1422 when Henry relented and ordered Joan's release and restitution (Henry died six weeks later). There is no doubt that the allegations were false and that Henry's motives were purely mercenary: to reduce the queen's expenses and pocket the surplus – some £8000 between June 1421 and August 1422 alone.

☆ FIRST official London hangman hanged

Cratwell (aka Gretwell), London. 1538

Four years after being appointed London's first official executioner, hangman Cratwell was hanged in front of 20,000 spectators for robbing a booth at St Bartholomew's Fair. Other notable London hangmen hanged include: Stump-leg, hanged for thieving in 1558; Pascha Rose, hanged for housebreaking and theft in 1686; and John Price, hanged for murdering an old woman in 1718.

✻ LAST person executed by the sword in England

Queen Anne Boleyn, Tower of London. c. 11:00 Friday 19 May 1536

Convicted of adultery and treason, Anne was sentenced 'to be burned alive or beheaded, at the King's pleasure'. The king chose beheading but, as Anne had suffered a morbid fear of the axe since childhood, she begged to die by the sword – a request Henry granted. A highly skilled French executioner was bought over from Calais; he was paid one hundred French crowns (about £23), which included payment for a tight-fitting black suit and a high horn-shaped hat attached to a half mask which covered the upper part of his face. Just after 11:00, Anne arrived at the straw-laden scaffold and removed her grey damask cloak to reveal a red underskirt. Her famously long black hair was held in place by a black cap which was removed and replaced by a simple white one. She prayed, declared her loyalty to Henry and was then blindfolded with a linen handkerchief. There was no block. She knelt, and as she did so the executioner silently withdrew the sword from where he had hidden it from her view under the straw. He signalled to his assistant to approach Anne who, hearing the footsteps, turned towards the sound. As she turned the sword swept down and with one clean stroke severed her head. With blood gushing everywhere the executioner held the head high and witnesses saw that Anne's eyes and lips were still moving convulsively. Her remains were placed in an old arrow chest and buried under the altar of the Chapel Royal of Peter ad Vincula within the Tower walls.

DID YOU KNOW?

Anne's headless ghost is said to haunt Blickling Hall in Norfolk, where it supposedly arrives every year on the anniversary of her death in a coach driven by a headless coachman.

❏ ONLY woman known to have been tortured on the rack

Anne Askew, Tower of London. Tuesday 29 June 1546

On 28 June 1546 Anne Askew, a close friend of Henry VIII's last wife Catherine Parr, was arraigned for heresy charged with trying to convert the queen into becoming a Protestant. Askew was condemned 'without any triall of a jurie' and the next day she was taken to the Tower of London where officials demanded she name other members of her 'secte'. When she refused, they took the exceptional step of having her tortured. She was taken to the White Tower where the Lord Chancellor Sir Thomas Wriothesley ordered her to be given the excruciating rack – even going so far as to turn the rack himself. As a woman, gently born, and a condemned person, she should have been exempt from such torture on three counts. Even under the agony of what is considered the most painful of all tortures she refused to answer their questions: 'quietly and patiently praying to the Lord, she endured their tyranny till her bones and joints were almost plucked asunder.' On 16 July, after two weeks in Newgate Prison, the 25-year-old was taken to Smithfield, strapped to a chair and burnt at the stake.

✳ LAST woman boiled alive in England

Margaret Davy, King's Lynn, Norfolk. Monday 28 March 1547

In 1531 Henry VIII added an extra refinement to the punishment for the offences of coining and poisoning – offenders were to be boiled to death. Sixteen years later, the last person to suffer this punishment was maidservant Margaret Davy, who had been convicted of multiple poisoning involving three families. At her execution a huge cauldron of water was placed in the marketplace and a fire lit beneath it to bring the water to boiling point. Attached by chains to a gantry above the pot, Margaret was repeatedly plunged in and out of the boiling water 'until life was extinct'.

☆ FIRST hangings on Tyburn's 'Triple Tree'

John Story et al, Tyburn, London. Friday 1 June 1571

The 'Triple Tree' was a triangular gallows eighteen feet high, with three beams each capable of holding eight victims – and on several occasions it was used to capacity, 24 victims all being hanged together. Whether it was designed to expedite criminals more efficiently or as an added attraction for the Tyburn Fair Days, which bought hundreds of extra visitors to the market, is debatable. The first victim was certainly a crowd pleaser. John Story, the first Regius Professor of Civil Law at Oxford, had been a notorious prosecutor of Protestants during the reign of Queen Mary I. After the accession of Elizabeth I he escaped to Flanders but was eventually captured and brought back to face punishment. Aged sixty, he was accused of conspiring to kill the queen and of providing military secrets to the Spanish. The 'Triple Tree' provided first-class entertainment on its debut when Story, while being disembowelled, hit back at the executioner – and the executioner revelled in taking his revenge.

☆ FIRST Head of State assassinated with a hand-gun

William the Silent, Prince of Orange, Holland. Friday 10 July 1584

Balthasar Gerard, a twenty-year-old religious zealot, went to William's avowedly Protestant court disguised as an impoverished Calvinist in search of alms. After William had given him twelve crowns Gerard, instead of leaving, hid in a corridor near William's dining room. Later that day he shot the prince three times with a wheel-lock pistol. William, who died within minutes, cried 'My God, have pity on my soul... Have pity on this poor people.' Gerard was captured while attempting to escape over a garden wall and his subsequent execution was one of the most gruesome on record. After first being tortured on the rack his right arm was burned off with a red-hot iron. His body was then flayed with red-hot pincers, his abdomen sliced open and his bowels ripped out before his legs and remaining arm were hacked off. Incredibly, he is reported to have still been alive until his heart was torn out and thrown in his face. It is said that Gerard remained totally silent throughout the agonising ordeal. Dutch Catholics, rejoicing in William's death, kept Gerard's head as a revered relic and sought to have him canonised.

✱ FIRST recorded arrival of female transportees in America

Virginia. Thursday 11 May 1609

Although taken from prisons these wretches were described as 'One hundred and forty maids'. Each was secured by an iron band attached to her legs, waist or ankles (sometimes all three) and fastened to a communal chain which meant that no one could move with dragging the others. On arrival they were sold at a slave auction against their weight in tobacco, fetching between 200 and 600 lbs of tobacco each, depending on their age and condition. The total number of women transported to the Americas in the eighteenth century exceeded 30,000; it was noted that while one-seventh of men died on the voyage, only half that proportion of women died because they were 'less impar'd by Drink'.

✱ LAST man burned at the stake in Britain

Edward Wightman, Lichfield. Saturday 11 April 1612

Anabaptist fanatic Edward Wightman, the last person burned for heresy in England, was actually burned twice! At first burning on 9 March the fire 'scorched him a little' and he cried out that he would recant. Thereupon the crowd rescued him, themselves getting 'scorched to save him'. A form of recantation was presented to him 'which he there read and professed, before he was unchained from the stake'. He was remitted to prison, where, for two or three weeks, he considered his captors' demand for a formal written recantation. He was brought once more to the consistory, where he refused to recant. Returned to the stake he reaffirmed his earlier views and died blaspheming 'more audaciously than before'.

☆ FIRST execution of a murderer in America

John Billington, Pilgrim Colony, Plymouth, Massachusetts. Thursday 30 September 1630

Fleeing England to escape creditors, America's first official murderer boarded the *Mayflower*, accompanied by his wife and two sons, as one of the original band of Pilgrim Fathers. In March 1621 Billington was convicted of contempt but escaped punishment, and in 1624 he was implicated in a failed revolt against the Plymouth church but again escaped punishment. Then, in September 1630, after a heated argument over hunting rights, Billington fatally shot fellow colonist John Newcomen with a blunderbuss: 'The poor fellow perceiving the intent of this Billington, his mortal enemy, sheltered himself behind trees as well as he could for a while; but the other, not being so ill a marksman as to miss his aim, made a shot at him, and struck him on the shoulder, with which he died soon after.' Billington was tried by jury hoping that 'either for want of power to execute for capital offences, or for want of people to increase the Plantation, he should have his life spared; but justice otherwise determined, and rewarded him, the first murtherer of his neighbor there, with the deserved punishment of death, for a warning to others.' He was hanged, his corpse left to rot and his skull reportedly nailed to a tree as grisly warning to others. Today many Americans proudly boast direct ancestry from Billington.

☆ FIRST complete record of a woman hanged in the American Colonies

Dorothy Talbye, Boston, Massachusetts. Monday 10 December 1638

Dorothy and her husband and four children barely scraped a living. At first she sought solace through the Church but soon became disillusioned and started behaving irrationally. She was twice punished for attacking her husband and finally, wracked by poverty and despair, she decided that her baby would be better off dead than alive so she broke its neck – her defence that she wanted to save the child from a life of poverty did not save her from the death penalty. She pleaded to die by axe rather than the rope but her wish was denied, and on the scaffold she wore a veil to spite the the spectators. She was forcibly dragged to the noose, fought while the executioners pinioned her, and finally shook the veil from her face and snarled at the crowd before being hanged.
(*Note: The first recorded hanging of a woman in America was that of Jane Champion, who was hanged in Virginia in 1632 for an unrecorded offence. Margaret Hatch was hanged in Virginia on 24 June 1633 for murder but there are no extant details of either execution.*)

❏ ONLY couple hanged for adultery in America

Mary Latham and James Britton, Colony of Massachusetts. Tuesday 21 March 1643

In 1641 the colony of Massachusetts made adultery a capital offence, based on the Ten Commandments. Eighteen-year-old Mary Latham was an attractive religious girl who fell in love with a local young man who jilted her. On the rebound she declared she would marry the first eligible man who proposed. He turned out to be three times her age. Unsurprisingly the union was deeply unhappy, and Mary quickly developed a relationship with thirty-year-old James Britton, a local free-living womaniser. Mary and James were seen leaving a party early and were observed having sex in the nearby woods. Arrested the following day they both admitted their guilt. After much dispute over the legality of the case their confessions were held sufficient to condemn them both. On the scaffold both made final speeches warning of the folly of sexual misconduct. The law remained in effect for many years but this is the only time adultery was punished by death in America.

✳ LAST victim of the Halifax Gibbet

Abraham Wilkinson and Antony Mitchell, Halifax. Tuesday 30 April 1650

The guillotine was in use in England long before it was 'invented' in France. First used in 1286 it operated in Halifax, Yorkshire, where by ancient prerogative the local council could administer its own laws. One of these was that any felon committing a crime netting more than thirteen and one half pence would be beheaded on the next market day. The method used was a locally designed and built machine nicknamed the Halifax Gibbet – a misleading name in that gibbet properly means an iron cage in which the corpse of an executed person was suspended. The Halifax Gibbet comprised two fifteen foot timber uprights joined at the top by a transverse beam; a blade measuring 10.5 x 9 inches and weighing 7lb 12oz ran in grooves cut into the uprights and was held at the top of the frame by a wooden pin attached to a long rope. A large number of locals would pull the rope so that no one person would be responsible for the felon's death. Should the stolen item be a cow, horse or similar animal, the rope would be tied to the beast which would be allowed to wander at leisure, leaving the actual moment of death as matter of agonising anticipation. Wilkinson and Mitchell, convicted of stealing sixteen yards of russett-coloured kersey (a coarse woollen cloth) and two horses, were the last two felons to face the Halifax Gibbet after 364 years' use. A replica of the machine can be seen in the Halifax Piece Hall Museum.

☆ FIRST independent police force
☆ FIRST chief of police

Gabriel Nicholas de la Reynie, Paris police force. March 1667

The formation of the Paris police force in 1667 from what had been part of the Royal Watch separated the dispensation of justice from the enforcement of the law for the first time, making Paris the first city to have an independent police force. The world's first police chief was de la Reynie, who served almost thirty years as Lieutenant-General of the newly formed force, from March 1667 to January 1697. As well as having authority over all existing institutions of law enforcement, de la Reynie also served as judge or prosecutor in lawsuits involving the aristocracy. These included the infamous murder scandal known as *L'Affair des Poisons* ('The Affair of the Poisons') which saw a number of aristocrats implicated for poisoning and witchcraft.(*See also First police station 1698*)

☆ FIRST victim of the Popish Plot
✳ LAST head publicly exhibited on London Bridge

William Staley, London Bridge. Tuesday 26 November 1678

The Popish Plot was an elaborate hoax by means of which Titus Oates and accomplices convinced the authorities that Catholics were plotting to assassinate Charles II. In London 2,000 Catholics were imprisoned, houses were searched, and unjust executions became daily events. On 14 November 1678 William Staley, a Catholic goldsmith and banker, happened to enter a pastrycook's shop in Covent Garden, where a man named Carstairs also stood. Carstairs subsequently tried to blackmail Staley, claiming that in the pastry-shop he had heard Staley threaten to kill the king. Staley refused to buy Carstairs' silence, whereupon Carstairs immediately had him arrested. At Staley's trial on 21 November Carstairs testified that he had heard Staley call the king 'a great Heretic and the greatest Rogue in the World' and that with hand on heart Staley had declared 'I would with this hand kill him myself'. Staley claimed that Carstairs had misconstrued a discussion regarding the king of France but the Lord Chief Justice dismissed this as 'a Jesuit's trick' and Staley was found guilty. Offered his life if he would reveal any further plots, Staley said that he neither knew of any plots nor had spoken the words he was accused of. On 26 November he was dragged on a sledge to Tyburn where he was hanged, drawn and quartered. But instead of his quarters being set upon the city gates the king allowed them to be delivered to his relatives. Mass was said over his remains and a 'grand' funeral was arranged from his father's house on 29 November, before his burial in St Paul's, Covent Garden. This incensed the government so much that the coroner ordered the body to be dug up and delivered to the sheriff. Staley's quarters were displayed on the City's gate and his head was set up on London Bridge, the last to be publicly exhibited there.

✳ LAST person decapitated by the Scottish Maiden

Archibald Campbell, 9th Earl of Argyll, Edinburgh, Scotland. Tuesday 30 June 1685

The Scottish Maiden was a simple copy of the Halifax Gibbet (*see 1650 above*), whose name 'Maiden' may be derived from the Celtic mod-dun, meaning 'place of justice'. It was introduced into Scotland in 1565 by the James Douglas, Earl of Morton, Regent of Scotland, who probably regretted his enterprise when on 2 June 1581 he was executed by it himself after his involvement in the murder of Lord Darnley, the husband of Mary Queen of Scots. The device decapitated over 120 victims including a father and son: Archibald Campbell, Marquis of Argyll, who was executed for treason on 27 May 1661; and his son the 9th Earl of Argyll (also called Archibald Campbell) who became its final victim on 30 June 1685. Just before the blade fell Argyll Jr kissed the infernal machine and called it 'the sweetest maiden I have ever kissed'.

✳ LAST Royal execution in Britain

James, Duke of Monmouth, London. Wednesday 15 July 1685

Monmouth, the eldest of Charles II's numerous bastards, lived in Holland and in 1685 attempted to claim the English throne from his uncle James II. His rebellion, the last popular uprising in England, culminated in the last pitched battle on English soil, the Battle of Sedgemoor, on 6 July 1685. Roundly beaten, Monmouth was eventually captured and taken before James II, with whom he pleaded, 'Remember, Sir, I am your brother's son and if you take my life, it is your own blood you will shed.' James was unmoved, and on 15 July Monmouth was taken to Tower Hill escorted by officers with strict orders to shoot him dead if he tried to escape.

At the black-draped scaffold Monmouth announced, 'I will make no speeches. I come to die.' He gave the executioner Jack Ketch six guineas saying, 'Pray do your business well; do not serve me as you did my Lord Russell. I have heard you struck him three or four times – if you strike me twice I cannot promise not to move.' He then promised Ketch a further six guineas if he did his job well. Removing his coat and wig and refusing a blindfold he tried his neck on the low block for size. Still concerned about Ketch's reputation for incompetence he asked Ketch, 'Prithee, let me feel the axe,' and having done so said, 'I fear it is not sharp enough.' Ketch gruffly replied, 'It is sharp and heavy enough.' Monmouth laid his head on the block. The first blow struck wide, only inflicting a flesh wound. Monmouth half raised himself, stared reproachfully at Ketch then quietly resumed his position. The second blow was equally ineffective, as was the third. At this point Ketch threw away the axe and offered his fee to anybody who would finish the job but the angry crowd threatened to tear Ketch to pieces unless he completed the task. After five strokes Monmouth's head still clung by sinews to the body and the final separation was completed by handknife. When it was realised that no official portrait existed of Monmouth his head was sewn back onto his body and Sir Godfrey Kneller painted him wearing a handsome neckscarf; the result is on permanent display in Britain's National Portrait Gallery.

☆ FIRST victim of Judge Jeffrey's Bloody Assizes

Lady Alice Lisle, Winchester. Wednesday 2 September 1685

The 71-year-old victim was executed for giving shelter to Methodist minister John Hicks and soldier Richard Nelthorpe, who had fought for the Duke of Monmouth in his failed rebellion of 1685. On 26 August, having been informed on by John Barter, a local labourer, the fugitives were apprehended and Lady Alice was charged with treason for harbouring Hicks. The following day Lady Alice became the first person to be tried before Lord Chief Justice George Jeffreys in what subsequently became known as the 'bloody assizes'. Aged, infirm, and nearly deaf, she needed a friend to stand close by her in court and repeat all that was said to her; she acknowledged hiding Hicks but rejected the charge of treason. However, the government clearly wished to make an example of her (Jeffreys commented, 'I would have condemned her had she been my mother') and after a gruelling six-hour trial, she was convicted and condemned by a reluctant jury to be burned alive; on appeal, King James reduced the sentence to beheading. In her dying speech, Lady Alice reiterated that her only crime was 'Entertaining a Non-Conformist Minister'. The public was shocked that a woman of her age and social standing should be executed while others, more fully implicated in the rebellion, received lesser sentences or pardons. However, at least one contemporary thought her sentence just. He wrote her epitaph:

> Here Lies Madam Lisle Dead,
> Which for Treason lost her Head,
> She Patroniz'd the Cause, The Cause,
> Against the Church and 'stablish'd Laws,
> Let all her sex both Great and small,
> Take here Example by her Fall,
> And henceforth ever shun to be
> Entangled by Presbiery.

While Jeffreys was probably technically correct in his decision, the excessive sentence cast a pall over the remaining trials and lent credence to the charge that she was the victim of judicial murder. Popular opinion overwhelmingly supported Alice Lisle, portraying her as a Protestant martyr and a victim of royal vindictiveness.

☆ FIRST 'Witch' executed at the Salem Witch Trials

Bridget Bishop, Salem, Massachusetts. Friday 10 June 1692

Sixty-year-old Bridget Bishop was the first of fourteen women, six men and two dogs to be executed during the hysteria of the Salem witchcraft trials. Of the twenty human executions, nineteen were hanged and one pressed to death; none were burned at the stake. A further 175 to 200 people were imprisoned, at least five of whom died in jail. The outspoken, unruly and flashily dressed Bridget Bishop had been married three times. Husband number one was George Wasselbe, who died at a young age; number two was businessman Thomas Oliver with whom she had one daughter, Christian. She was accused of bewitching Thomas Oliver to death but was acquitted for lack of evidence. Her last marriage was to Edward Bishop, a sawyer whose family ran a prosperous tavern in Beverly. He signed an affidavit against her, but his own son and daughter-in-law were also taken to jail on charges of witchcraft only days before Bridget's arrest. Bridget denied all charges of witchcraft, saying, 'I know not what a witch is.'

DID YOU KNOW?

One of the women accused of witchcraft in seventeenth-century Salem, Massachusetts, was named Margaret Thatcher. Other crime-associated figures with more famous namesakes include Norman Schwarzkopf, the police officer in charge of the Lindbergh kidnapping investigation; Bernard Shaw, a bodyguard who married Patty Hearst after her kidnapping; and armed robber Charles Bronson, the UK's most violent prisoner, who changed his name by deed poll from Michael Peterson to that of his film-star hero.

❏ ONLY person to be pressed to death in America

Giles Corey, Salem, Massachusetts. Monday 19 September 1692

Pressing (*peine forte et dure*) was punishment for any prisoner who refused to plead, and consisted of placing weights one by one on the victim until the pain forced him or her to answer the charge. The significance was that if a person failed to plead he couldn't be tried and convicted and therefore his possessions could not be confiscated. Eighty-year-old Giles Corey (aka Cory) had been caught up in the hysteria of the Salem witchhunt, even accusing his own wife, but when he was himself accused he recognised the madness of it all and protested by contemptuous silence. Realising that he could save his property if not his life, he refused to plead at his trial and was dragged into the field next to the jail. He was spreadeagled naked, his ankles and wrists tied to stakes, and a rough wooden board the size of a door placed over him. As more stones were added he refused to say anything other than 'More weight' so that he might die sooner. His ribs cracked, his intestines burst and lungs were crushed. In extremis Corey's tongue involuntarily protruded from his mouth; the sheriff used his cane to push it back. He suffered for two days before dying and his courage is credited with building the public revulsion that finally ended the witchcraft trials.

☆ FIRST police uniforms

New York. 8 July 1693

Authorised by the Common Council of New York, ordering the mayor to provide the police 'with a coat of the city livery, with the badge of the city arms, shoes and stockings, and charge it to the account of the city'.

☆ FIRST police station

Pont-Neuf, Paris. 1698

After the Paris police force was formed as the world's first (*see 1667*) the force continued to operate from Le Petit Châtelet ('the little castle') near Pont-au-Change, which was also the base of the judiciary from which the police had just been separated. Then, in 1698, the new chief of police Marquis d'Argenson moved his force to new headquarters close to Pont Neuf, which effectively became the world's first police station.

✳ LAST person convicted in England of being a witch

Jane Wenham, Hertford. Saturday 4 March 1721

Twice married and twice widowed, Wenham had a reputation for swearing, cursing, idleness, thievery and whoredom. Early in 1712 farmer John Chapman blamed her for a spate of deaths among his livestock and claimed that she had bewitched his farmhand. Wenham sued for defamation and the adjudicator, Reverend Gardiner (who believed in witches), ordered Chapman to pay just one shilling compensation. Wenham muttered, 'If I can't have justice here I shall have it elsewhere,' and the threat was not forgotten. When Gardiner's servant Ann Thorne was subsequently afflicted with terrible fits and delusions, Wenham was arrested. Her body was searched for witches' marks but none were found so, to prove her innocence, she was asked to recite the Lord's Prayer as it was believed that no witch could do so. Unfortunately she faltered during the recitation. Her lodgings were searched and an ointment was found under her pillow which prosecutors claimed was made from the fat of melted corpses. Wenham's trial, on 4 March 1712 before the sympathetic Sir John

Powell, became a battle of lawyers versus clergy. The only indictment which the assize lawyers would accept was that she had conversed with the devil in the form of a cat. When the prosecution claimed she could fly Powell remarked as far as he knew there was no law against flying. However, sixteen witnesses gave accounts of how she had bewitched them and she was found guilty. Against his better judgement Powell was forced to sentence her to death by hanging but he then personally obtained a reprieve and, shortly afterwards, a royal pardon. Wenham left the village but Anne Thorne continued to have visions of the devil as a cat. Thorne was ordered to wash her hands and face twice daily and be watched over by a 'lusty young fellow,' which worked – she recovered and married him.

DID YOU KNOW?

Jane Wenham's case (*above*) became a cause célèbre, and she was visited by the Revd (later Bishop) Francis Hutchinson. Her story inspired Hutchinson to write his 'Historical Essay Concerning Witchcraft' – an active exposé of witch hunters which was credited with suppressing the superstition in England.

❏ ONLY persons executed under the bizarre Coventry Act

Arundel Coke and John Woodburne, Bury St Edmunds, Suffolk. Saturday 31 March 1722

The Coventry Act stated that a man could be executed for lying in wait and deliberately disfiguring a victim – especially by putting out an eye, disabling the tongue or slitting the nose. The Act was created after the heavy-drinking politician Sir John Coventry was attacked in Covent Garden in December 1670 after insulting King

Charles II in the House of Commons. Coventry was arguing for a tax on theatres, and when Sir John Berkenhead commented that theatres had been of great service to the king, Coventry promptly asked if Berkenhead meant the male or female players. This was an obvious reference to the king's two mistresses, the actresses Nell Gwyn and Moll Davies. That same night Coventry and his young servant were viciously attacked by members of the Duke of Monmouth's troop, led by Sir Thomas Sandys, and Coventry's nose was slit to the bone. MPs were so affronted that early in 1671 they passed an Act in Coventry's honour, 'to prevent malicious maiming and wounding'. The only prosecution under this act came after barrister Arundel Coke botched a plot to kill his brother-in-law Edwin Crispe, on whose death he was due to inherit a substantial sum of money. On 1 January 1722 Coke and Crispe went to visit a local woman, Mistress Monke, and after they parted John Woodburne brutally attacked Crispe with a billhook, slitting his nose but failing to kill him. Crispe voiced his suspicions that Coke was involved, and two men (a tailor named Moon and a blacksmith named Carter) informed police that Coke had tried to hire them to kill Crispe. Coke was arrested and confessed, complaining if Woodburne had cut Crispe's throat as he had been paid to do, and 'not been a cow-hearted dog', Crispe could never have testified against him. Coke paid to be hanged quietly at 06:00, but Woodburne was hanged later in front of a huge crowd at Tayfen Meadows.

DID YOU KNOW?

The Coventry Act was not repealed until 1828. Coventry recovered from the attack, and his wounds were not permanent – which was fortunate because he needed his sense of smell after 1660, when he was appointed a commissioner for sewers in Somerset.

* **LAST** man executed by the axe
- **ONLY** prisoner of both the Bastille and the Tower of London

Simon Fraser, Lord Lovat, Tower Hill, London. Thursday 9 April 1747

For his part in the 1745 Jacobite Rebellion eighty-year-old Lovat was condemned to death by the axe: a method of beheading reserved for the nobility. As he was awaiting execution a nearby scaffold collapsed killing eight or ten spectators (including the master carpenter of the scaffold and his wife who were selling beer underneath it); with laughing approval Lovat remarked, 'The more mischief the better the sport.' He displayed no fear and 'looked death in the face with a smiling Countenence', putting on his spectacles to check the inscription on his coffin. He was extremely fat and reputed to possess the shortest neck in Scotland, prompting speculation as to whether the axeman could do his job at a single blow – to make sure he did, the executioner swung so hard that Lovat's head flew from his body and the axe-blade was buried two inches deep in the block. The axe and the block can both still be seen in the Tower of London. By curious coincidence, the first man to be beheaded at Tower Hill was also an eighty-year-old by the name of Simon: Simon of Sudbury, Archbishop of Canterbury, who was seized by Wat Tyler's rebels and beheaded on a makeshift log acting as a block.

DID YOU KNOW?

Although Lovat (*above*) was the last person in England to die by beheading he was not the last to be beheaded. A dozen or more lost their their heads after they were dead – sentenced to die by hanging, drawing and quartering (which wasn't abolished by Parliament until 1870) or by hanging and beheading. (*See 1820*)

* **LAST** person executed in Scotland for bestiality
* **LAST** use of burning as a method of execution in
Scotland

*Alexander Geddes, Castlehill, Aberdeen, Scotland. 05:00 Tuesday
25 June 1751*

Geddes, a farmer from Kinnermony in Banffshire, was known to
have indulged in bestiality for some fifteen years. In 1751 he was
found guilty of 'reiterated acts of the monstrous crime of bestiality
with a mare'. At dawn on 25 June that year he was taken to Castlehill,
where he was hanged on the gibbet, cut down alive and burned.

☆ **FIRST** poison trial to feature decisive toxicological
testimony

Mary Blandy, Oxford Assizes. Friday 3 March 1752

Blandy lived with her father Frances, a prosperous lawyer who had
promised her a dowry of £10,000. In September 1747 the
Honorable Captain William Henry Cranstoun began courting
Mary. Although Cranstoun was small, pock-marked, cross-eyed,
and 46 years old to Mary's 26, she was enamoured. But her father
discovered Cranstoun was already married and banished him
from the house. Undaunted, Cranstoun promised to divorce his
wife and sent Mary some white powder, saying that if she gave it
secretly to her father it would sweeten him towards the match.
Innocently (or so she later claimed) Mary began to administer the
powder. Mr Blandy began to suffer stomach pains, and on 14
August 1751 he died in agony, complaining that there was a
fireball inside him. Mary was arrested and Cranstoun fled to
France, where he died seven months later. At Mary's trial on 3
March 1752 four doctors testified that Blandy's stomach and

intestines were 'prodigiously inflamed and excoriated' and his internal organs were discoloured and marked with bruise-like spots but well preserved – all consistent with arsenic poisoning. Despite claiming she believed the powder was a love potion Mary the jury took just five minutes to find her guilty. She was publicly hanged at 09:00 on 6 April 1752, dressed in black and with her hands bound in black ribbon, still proclaiming her innocence. She was also concerned, in those knickerless days, that men beneath the gallows would peer up her skirt, and her last words were to the executioner: 'Do not hang me too high, for the sake of decency.' Ironically, Mr Blandy may have brought about his own death – the £10,000 dowry never existed; it was a trap to lure a rich suitor.

☆ FIRST victim to be hanged and anatomised

Thomas Wilford, Tyburn, London. Thursday 22 June 1752

At the age of seventeen, one-armed Thomas Wilford met 22-year-old Sarah Williams, a 'girl of ill-fame'. She beguiled him into marriage, knowing that the churchwardens would give them money to start their married life. Their wedding duly took place on Monday 29 May 1752 and Williams collected £2. The following Sunday she stayed out till midnight, and when Wilford asked where she'd been she said, 'To the park.' A violent row ensued, during which Wilford seized a knife, threw her down and, kneeling on her, cut her throat so that her head was almost severed. He immediately confessed to another lodger: 'I have murdered my poor wife, whom I loved as dearly as my own life.' At his Old Bailey trial he was told: 'You stand convicted of the horrid and unnatural crime of murdering Sarah, your wife. This Court doth adjudge that you be taken back to the place from whence you came, and there to be fed on bread and water till Wednesday next, when you are to be taken to the common place of execution, and there hanged by the neck until you are dead; after which your body is to be publicly dissected and anatomised, agreeable to an Act of Parliament in that case made and provided; and may God Almighty have mercy on your soul!' Wilford's corpse was the first to be dissected and anatomised under a new Act of Parliament intended to provide surgeons with a ready supply of cadavers for research.

☆ FIRST person hanged using the 'drop' method
❊ LAST English nobleman to suffer a 'felon's death' (executed by hanging as opposed to beheading)
❑ ONLY peer of the realm hanged for murder
❑ ONLY time the 'drop' was used at Tyburn

Laurence Shirley, 4th Earl Ferrers, Tyburn. Monday 5 May 1760

Ferrers had a history of violence which, on 18 January 1760, culminated in murder. After unjustly accusing his steward John Johnson of conniving to deprive him of a lucrative coal-mining contract, Ferrers made Johnson kneel before him, yelled, 'Your time is come, you must die!', then shot him in the stomach. Johnson died seventeen hours later. Tried by his peers in the House of Lords, Ferrers pleaded unsound mind but was found guilty and sentenced to death. He asked to be beheaded, as was his right as a nobleman, but was refused. Ferrers was driven to Tyburn in his own landau, wearing his white wedding suit embroidered with silver – though his ex-wife had divorced him for 'unwarrantable cruelty'. Seeing the size of the crowd Ferrers surmised, 'They never saw a Lord hanged before.' He stood on the collapsible platform (a precursor of the trap door) wearing a white cap and with his arms bound by a black sash. The eighteen-inch drop, designed to break Ferrer's neck rather than strangle him, was too short, leaving his toes touching the boards; he took four minutes to die, even with the executioner and his assistant tugging his legs to hasten his demise. The corpse was anatomised at Surgeons' Hall and then put on public display for three days before being given a family burial. As the 'drop' was deemed a failure, subsequent Tyburn executions were carried out either by 'step-off' or by the traditional horse and cart method, and the drop didn't become general practice until 1783.

* LAST witch executed in Europe

Anna Maria Schwagel, Kempten, Bavaria. Tuesday 11 April 1775

Schwagel worked in service for a wealthy family in Lachen, Bavaria, where she became infatuated with the coachman who generously offered to deflower the 30-something virgin on condition she renounce her Catholic faith. She agreed, but he then abandoned her. The triple shock of losing her virginity, her faith and her lover led her to seek absolution from an Augustinian friar – but when the friar subsequently converted to Protestantism Schwagel became convinced that only the devil could have so evilly double-crossed her. Some time later she was found in a crazed state, walking the streets dressed in rags and begging for alms. She was taken to an asylum in Laneggen, near Kempten, where she told other inmates that she was a lapsed Catholic who had abandoned her faith to a Satanist lover with whom she had attended sabbats and indulged in obscene activities. Her constant murmuring, 'It was the Devil in the form of the coachman who betrayed me,' led everyone to believe that her lover was in fact the Devil himself. The story reached the ears of the matron, Anna Maria Kuhstaller, who beat Schwagel into confessing that she'd had intercourse with the Devil and then denounced Schwagel to local magistrates. She was arrested on 20 February 1775, found guilty of witchcraft and beheaded on 11 April 1775.

☆ FIRST recorded parking legislation

Westminster, London. Wednesday 29 November 1775

Laws made at Westminster governed the daily life of the residents of Dorchester in Dorset. In 1775 Parliament made it law that any person who left a horse and cart longer than necessary for unloading would 'forfeit the sum of five shillings'. Failure to pay would result in offenders' 'carts, wagons, drays or other carriages' being towed away and locked up in a local pound.

☆ FIRST woman executed by Americans, as distinct from the British
✱ LAST public hanging in the Commonwealth
☆ FIRST capital case tried in American jurisdiction in Massachusetts
☆ FIRST case of a capital offence under the new US Constitution

Bathsheba Spooner, Worcester, Massachusetts. Thursday 2 July 1778

Bathsheba Spooner is probably the most socially prominent American woman ever to have been executed. Beautiful, well-educated and wealthy, she was the daughter of a chief justice of the Massachusetts Court. She was also a liar, schemer, adulteress and child-seducer. At the age of nineteen she married 56-year-old Joshua Spooner, a wealthy retired merchant, and in 1778, aged thirty-two, she took sixteen-year-old Ezra Ross as a lover. She plotted with Ross to murder Spooner by paying two British deserters, James Buchanan and William Brooks, to help kill him. On the night of 1 March 1778 the three men attacked Spooner outside his home, throttled him, then threw his unconscious body down a well. The corpse was soon discovered and Buchanan and Brooks were found a few days later wearing Spooner's clothes – all four conspirators were sentenced to death. Bathsheba begged for mercy on the grounds that she was pregnant, and was examined by 'two men midwives and twelve discreet lawful matrons' who unanimously declared that she was not with child. A second examination resulted in the same diagnosis and she was hanged alongside her lover and two accomplices – a rare quadruple hanging which attracted a crowd of some 5,000 people. Bathsheba's last request was a full autopsy, which revealed 'a perfectly developed male foetus aged between five and six months'. It is believed the midwives' false diagnosis was politically motivated, because Bathsheba was a Royalist sympathiser while they were all staunch revolutionaries.

☆ FIRST American prisoner in the Tower of London

Henry Laurens, Tower of London. Friday 6 October 1780

Laurens, former president of the American Congress, was captured while sailing to Holland to make a treaty on behalf of the American States, and letters he threw overboard were recovered and led to the British declaration of war against Holland on 20 December 1780. As the American War of Independence was still raging Laurens was taken by the British 'on suspicion of high treason', and incarcerated in two small rooms in the Tower. He was obliged to pay rent and provide his own meat, drink, bedding, coals and candles. He was also asked to pay £100 to the warders for their attendance but refused to do so, claiming it wasn't he who was employing them! The British desperately tried to win him over, even threatening him with hanging, but he stayed true to his cause and, despite close guard, frequently smuggled out communications to the rebel press. Laurens was eventually released on 31 December 1781, after 451 days confinement, in exchange for the British commander Lord Cornwallis who had surrendered to George Washington at Yorktown. Ironically Cornwallis was still officially Constable of the Tower of London.

✳ LAST execution at Tyburn

John Austen (aka Austin) hanged by Ned Dennis, Tyburn. Friday 7 November 1783

The dubious honour of being the last of over 50,000 people executed at Tyburn fell to John Austin, who had been found guilty of robbing John Spicer and wounding him 'in a cruel manner'. Austen was hanged by Edward Dennis, who charged six shillings and eightpence per hanging. On this occasion Dennis botched the execution by driving the cart from under Austin while he was still mid-prayer – and, having placed the halter in the wrong position, he left Austin performing a death dance until he finally succumbed.

DID YOU KNOW?

Not everyone was keen to break the 600-year Tyburn tradition. Dr Johnson said: 'No Sir, it is not an improvement; they object that the old method drew together a number of spectators. Sir, executions are intended to draw spectators. If they don't draw spectators, they don't answer their purpose. The old method was most satisfactory to all parties: the public was gratified by a procession: the criminal was supported by it. Why is this all to be swept away?' The answer was simple – the best quarter of London had extended to Tyburn and the new residents hated the disruption of executions. In the 600 years of its existence Tyburn became the generic name for a place of public execution and was adopted in other cities including Liverpool, York and Dublin.

* FIRST hangings outside Newgate Prison in the Old Bailey

Old Bailey, London. Tuesday 9 December 1783

After the demise of Tyburn (*see 1783 left*) the new site for public hanging in the City of London or the County of Middlesex was a scaffold in front of the Debtor's Door of Newgate Prison in the Old Bailey. To make way for the new venue many houses which had divided the Old Bailey into two narrow lanes were demolished, making it one broad thoroughfare as it is today. The new gallows was stored in a shed within Newgate Prison and produced on demand. The great advantage over Tyburn was that the new scaffold incorporated a trap door, fastened by a bolt, on which the prisoner stood. Once pulled the victims dropped through the trap up to their knees in the hope of mercifully dislocating their necks rather than allowing them to slowly strangle to death. As well as being the last hangman at Tyburn Edward (Ned) Dennis became the first at Newgate. He and his assistant William Brunskill successfully hanged ten people on the first day of executions, although the new gallows could actually accommodate twenty victims at a single event.

☆ FIRST murderer executed after being trapped by 'scientific detection'

William Richardson, Dumfries, Scotland. Saturday 30 June 1787

Richardson cut the throat of his nineteen-year-old lover Elizabeth Hughan, who was seven months pregnant. Doctors ruled out suicide and concluded that since the cut was from the right to the left, the murderer must have been left-handed. Although it was midsummer and the ground hard, a trail of footprints was found in boggy ground near the cottage where Elizabeth lived with her parents. The tracks revealed that the person had been running and had at one point slipped and been immersed up to his knee. Blood was also found on a stile. Plaster casts of the footprints were taken, revealing that the shoes were shod with iron nails and had recently been repaired. Police measured the footwear of all the men who attended the funeral; not only did Richardson's shoe match the impression but he was also found to be left-handed. His alibi seemed solid until his companions recalled that he had visited the blacksmith alone, was gone much longer than anticipated, and had returned with muddy stockings and a scratch on his cheek. A search of his cottage turned up the muddied stockings hidden in the thatch, and the clincher was that the mud on the stockings contained sand found only in the bog near Hughan's cottage. Faced with all this evidence, Richardson confessed and was hanged on 30 June 1787. His corpse was given to surgeons to aid scientific research.

☆ FIRST execution in Australia

Thomas Barrett, Sydney Cove, New South Wales. 18:30 Wednesday 27 February 1788

Barrett was hanged for the theft of butter, pease and pork. A convict volunteered to act as executioner but lost his nerve and refused to carry it out, even on pain of being shot by the Marines, and eventually the hanging was performed by Provost-Marshal Midshipman Henry Brewer. Records state that, 'Just before Barrett was turned off, he confessed the justice of his sentence, and that he had led a very wicked life... He then exhorted all [other convicts] to take warning by his unhappy fate and so launched into Eternity.'

❑ ONLY American female pirate executed

Rachel Wall, Boston, Massachusetts. Thursday 8 October 1789

After stealing a ship together at Essex, New England, Rachel joined her husband George in a life of piracy. Pretending to be in distress, Rachel would stand on deck dressed as a man and cry for help. When rescuers arrived, George and his men would kill them, take any valuables, and sink their ship. In 1782 George drowned in a storm but Rachel was rescued and returned to Boston where she continued to steal from the cabins of ships docked in Boston Harbour. She was eventually convicted of murdering a sailor, and a wagon was specially built to hang her and two other criminals. It is ironic that as America's only known woman pirate she was executed not for piracy at sea but for robbery and murder on land.

☆ FIRST inmate admitted to Littledean Jail

Joseph Marshall, Littledean, Gloucestershire. Friday 18 November 1791

Marshall, a nineteen-year-old labourer, was imprisoned at Littledean for stealing a spade. A revolutionary House of Correction, Littledean was later used as the template for London's Pentonville Prison and for the Philadelphian Cherry Hill Penitentiary System in America. Sergeant Samuel Beard, the first Gloucestershire policeman to be killed in the line of duty, was stationed at Littledean Jail, and Ellen Howard, the last woman in Gloucestershire to be charged with witchcraft, was tried here in 1906 and found not guilty. After 1854 the jail became a police station, remand prison and, later, a petty sessional court. In 1974 it was the location for the film *House of Whipcord*. In 2003 Andy Jones turned into the 'Crime Through Time Museum', housing an outstanding collection of true crime material and curiosities.

☆ FIRST execution by guillotine

Nicolas-Jacques Pelletier, Place de Greve, Paris, France. Wednesday 25 April 1792

The guillotine began its 189-year career with the decapitation of a red-shirted highwayman Nicolas-Jacques Pelletier by the public executioner Charles-Henri Sanson, who had already practised on the corpses of criminals. Although the machine is named after Dr Joseph-Ignace Guillotin he did not invent it. Seeking to make executions as humane as possible he simply proposed reforms, urging the French government to adopt painless beheading 'achieved by means of a simple mechanism' as a humane method of execution for all convicted criminals, not just aristocrats, arguing that loss of life, rather than the pain inflicted while losing it, should constitute sufficient punishment. The first 'Guillotine' was designed by Dr Antoine Louis, the septuagenarian secretary of the Academy of Surgery, and built by the state carpenter and scaffold specialist Monsieur Guidon, incorporating ideas from various beheading machines that had been in use for over 500 years. The judge sentencing Pelletier announced that, 'The condemned will have nothing to endure but the apprehension of death, which apprehension will be more painful to you than the blow that robs you of life.' But Pelletier wasn't convinced, and had to be dragged to the scaffold in a fainting fit. However, his decapitation was so smooth that Dr Guillotin (*see Did You Know? opposite*) was convinced that 'The victim did not suffer at all. He was conscious of no more than a slight chill on the neck.' Sadly it was not a crowd pleaser. The bloodthirsty mob was so angry at the efficient decapitation, during which they had seen virtually nothing, that people started chanting, 'Bring me back my wooden gallows.' Legend has it that the humanitarian Dr Guillotin never attended an execution and hated having his name associated with the machine.

DID YOU KNOW?

The most exquisite refinement to the guillotine belonged to neither Dr Louis nor Dr Guillotin. Originally they both approved a crescent-shaped blade. The super-efficient slanting blade was the idea of none other than King Louis XVI who was to become its most famous victim. Guillotin himself died more prosaically of a carbuncle in the shoulder compounded by pneumonia.

✱ LAST victim of the ducking stool in England

Jenny Pipes, Leominster. 1809

The ducking stool was used for punishing scolds and gossips – a 'Shaming of the Shrew' achieved by a wooden chair on the end of a long seesawing beam. Victims were paraded around the streets before being tied in the chair, lifted high above the jeering crowd, and then plunged into a river or pond a number of times ranging from one warning dip to several (usually three) for regular offenders. Jenny Pipes, née Corran, nagged her husband so severely about their poverty that her brother-in-law, in whose house they were living, reported her to the local magistrates. Sentenced to the ducking stool, the route of her disgrace led past Jenny's home and down to the banks of the Kenwater River. To cries of 'Duck the scold' she was submerged in the icy water twice. Clearly the punishment wasn't effective because she immediately started cursing the magistrate who had sentenced her. This, the last ducking stool to be used in England, can be found in the Priory Church, Leominster. Jenny Pipes was the last to be ducked but not the last to be sentenced to ducking. Eight years later, in 1817, town councillors sentenced one Sarah Locke to the same punishment. She was wheeled around the town but wasn't ducked because the local pond was found to be too low.

☆ FIRST full-time professional detective

Eugène François Vidocq, HQ 6 Petite-rue-Sainte-Anne (now rue Boileau), Paris. 1811

Vidocq was an unlikely candidate to be the first head of the French Sûreté (Security). As a child he stole from his father, was imprisoned while still at school, then worked as an acrobat and a soldier before being sentenced to eight years as a galley slave for forgery. He escaped three times from the galleys at Brest, joined a band of highwaymen, betrayed them to the police, and in 1808 offered his services as a police informer. After achieving sensational results, he suggested the formation of a plainclothes unit and in 1811 the Brigade de Sûreté was established with Vidocq as its chief – the first full-time salaried member of a regular police force engaged solely on detective work. He began with just four men but eventually directed a force of twenty-eight detectives, all former criminals. A master of disguise and surveillance, he was brilliantly successful, and in one two-year period alone he captured nearly 1,000 crooks. Widely acknowledged as the father of modern criminal investigation, Vidocq's innovations included introducing record keeping (a card-index system), criminalistics and the science of ballistics into police work; he was among the first to make systematic use of plaster-of-paris casts of foot/shoe impressions (*see 30 June 1787*); and his form of anthropometrics is still partially used by French police. He also held patents on indelible ink and unalterable bond paper, and in 1833 he founded the first modern private detective agency and credit bureau, Le Bureau des Renseignements (*see 1833*). Most of what we know about Vidocq's astounding adventures comes from his own Memoires, whose veracity should be considered in light of the fact that eleven women attended his funeral, each clutching a different version of his will.

DID YOU KNOW?

Vidocq was a confidant of at least two famous contemporary French writers and an inspiration for many other writers around the world. Victor Hugo based not one but two characters in *Les Miserables* on Vidocq – both Jean Valjean and Inspector Javert. Honoré Balzac's character Vautran, in *Pere Goriot*, was also modelled after him. Vidocq was Emile Gaboriau's inspiration for his fictional detective Monsieur Lecoq, one of the first scientific and methodical investigators. Vidocq's legendary crime-solving reputation was also lauded in Poe's *Murders in the Rue Morgue* and in Herman Melville's *Moby Dick*. The fugitive in Charles Dickens' *Great Expectations* was also inspired by Vidocq's real-life exploits.

☆ FIRST specially-trained dog used for law enforcement

Moors near Midmar Lodge, Aberdeenshire, Scotland. Thursday 8 February 1816

In 1816 one of Scotland's most famous excisemen, Revenue Officer Malcolm Gillespie, bought a black and tan bull terrier to assist with his dangerous work catching smugglers. Gillespie trained the dog to seize horses by the nose and make them 'dance about' until they spilt their illicit loads. On the night of 8 February 1816 the dog proved its worth when for the first time it was set loose against a gang of whisky smugglers and their four pack horses – it attacked the terrified horses which reared and shed the whisky kegs they were carrying. The dog had been expensive but Gillespie prized it so highly that he 'would not have disposed of it for 100 guineas'. One drawback was that it attacked any horse with a load and refused to quit until the goods were thrown off or in possession of its master, but he also continued with genuine law enforcement, one notable success taking place at Cowtown of Kintore, where 'a deal of bloodshed occurred on both sides'. Sadly the following year, during a skirmish with smugglers at Parkhill on the banks of the River Don, Britain's first canine law enforcer was killed by a shot 'promiscuously fired in a preliminary skirmish while he stood by, muzzled, waiting his part in the play'. (*Gillespie also achieved a notable last: see 16 November 1827.*)

✳ LAST culprit hanged in Scotland for stealing a sheep

John Ritchie, Aberdeen. Friday 5 June 1818

Sheep stealing was so common in nineteenth-century Scotland that the jury recommended mercy but Ritchie was nonetheless sentenced to hang for stealing thirty sheep from the grounds of Gordon Castle. He celebrated his seventeenth birthday in the death cell, and on the scaffold he looked so young that many spectators walked away, unable to watch a child hang.

☆ FIRST treadmill designed for punishment

Bury St Edmonds County Goal, Suffolk. November 1819

The prison treadmill, aka treadwheel, was the brainchild of William Cubitt (later Sir William Cubitt) an engineer from Ipswich in Suffolk. In 1818 he patented a type of treadwheel where prison inmates walked around the exterior of the cylinder on a series of steps. This was different from the standard treadwheel where people walked around the interior or along the edge of the wheel, a system which had been used throughout the Middle Ages as motive power for the huge cranes used to build cathedrals and remove cargo from ships. Britain's 1779 Penitentiary Act allowed labour to be 'of the hardest and most servile Kind, in which Drudgery is chiefly required... such as treading in a wheel, or drawing in a Capstern, for turning a Mill or other Machine or Engine'. Cubitt's machine was perfect and was rapidly adopted throughout the prison system. Since the agonising labour needed to turn the wheel achieved absolutely nothing it was commonly known as 'grinding the wind'.

* LAST official beheadings in England

Arthur Thistlewood, Richard Tidd, James Inges, William Davidson and Arthur Brunt, Newgate. 06:08 Monday 1 May 1820

These conspirators were beheaded after they had been hanged (*see also 1747*). Thistlewood led a small band of terrorists who intended to kill members of Lord Liverpool's Tory cabinet at a private dinner in February 1820 and overthrow the government. But they had been infiltrated by a government spy and at their final meeting they were ambushed by Bow Street Runners. Three of the gang were sentenced to transportation but Thistlewood and four other ringleaders were sentenced to die traitors' deaths by being hanged then beheaded. The scaffold was covered in black cloth and spread with sawdust. Five lidless coffins were placed by the ropes alongside a chopping block. All five conspirators were amazingly collected on the scaffold, sucking oranges and making quips: Thistlewood reminded his comrades, 'We shall soon know the last grand secret'; Tidd was so keen he tripped on the scaffold steps, recovered himself and received an ovation; and Brunt pleased the crowd by taking a pinch of snuff and kicking off his shoes into the audience. Then the bolt was drawn and within five minutes all appeared dead. They hung for half an hour before a man appeared, wearing a dark hat pulled low, with a black mask and a coloured handkerchief hiding his face and mouth. The crowd booed and hissed as he severed the heads of the corpses with a small surgical knife, which took one hour and eight minutes. As each head was removed the assistant executioner held it high and proclaimed 'This is the head of (name), a traitor.' Instead of being held aloft by the forelock, Tidd's balding head had to be lifted two-handed by the cheeks; Davidson's bled profusely, and Brunt's was accidentally dropped, enraging the crowd as the head rolled about on the scaffold.

* LAST beheadings in Britain
* LAST execution for high treason in Scotland
* LAST to be sentenced to hanging, drawing and quartering (later reduced to hanging and quartering)

Andrew Hardie and John Baird, Broad Street, Stirling, Scotland. 14:49 Friday 8 September 1820

Baird and Hardie were executed for being ringleaders in a failed insurrection which took place in Glasgow on 1-2 April 1820. A crowd of 6,000 watched as Hardie mounted the scaffold and addressed the gallows with 'Hail! harbinger of eternal rest.' Both men wanted to make last political statements but the sheriff threatened to start the execution immediately if they did, so instead Hardie spoke of his religious beliefs. After they had been hooded Hardie seized Baird's hand and they dropped through the trap hand-in-hand. After the bodies had hung for half an hour the headsman – a delicate, young man of about twenty who wore black crêpe over his face – began his gruesome task. Using axe and block it took three strokes to sever Hardie's head and two to decapitate Baird. Twenty-seven years later, with the Home Secretary's permission, Baird's and Hardie's bodies were exhumed from Stirling and carried to Glasgow where they were given honourable burials and a memorial in Sighthill Cemetery.

☆ FIRST identification parade on record

Life Guards Barracks, London. 14:00 Monday 20 August 1821

On 7 August 1821 the death of Queen Caroline split the country, many people blaming her death, only nineteen days after being locked out of her own coronation, on stress caused by the callous behaviour of King George IV. Prime Minister Lord Liverpool, fearing her funeral on 14 August could be the catalyst for violent demonstrations, ordered the 1st Regiment of the Life Guards to escort the cortege through London's side streets rather than through the main thoroughfares. At Oxford Street barricades blocked the path of the cortege. Shots rang out and two men, Richard Hanney (aka Hannay or Honey) and George Francis, were killed. At the inquest one witness, William Alexander, claimed he saw an officer shoot Hanney and that 'I should know if I was to see him again, from a hundred others.' The jury asked the coroner to arrange for the witnesses to inspect the soldiers, dressed in the same way and riding the same horses as they were on the day of the killing. Seven witnesses made direct identifications, including Alexander, who was quite adamant as to the culprit. However, all of the soldiers denied any involvement and the coroner returned a verdict of 'Murder by an officer to the jury unknown.' Thus the first identity parade ended with the identified culprit unpunished.

✳ LAST person executed for forgery in Scotland

Malcolm Gillespie, Aberdeen. Friday 16 November 1827

As Scotland's most successful exciseman (and the second most famous, after Robbie Burns), Gillespie spent 27 years as the scourge of smugglers bringing contraband from the Continent. It was dangerous work, and he was injured at least 42 times by smugglers – but he also achieved a celebrity which encouraged him to live a lifestyle well beyond his means. His wife and twenty children were lavishly waited on by servants, and to pay for this Gillespie and his private secretary, George Edwards, forged and circulated 22 different bills with a total value of 554 pounds and 10 shillings; Gillespie also burned down his house in an attempt to collect insurance money. On 30 April 1827 Gillespie and Edwards were tried at the Circuit Court in Aberdeen. Edwards was found guilty of just one charge and sentenced to transportation but Gillespie was sentenced to death on eight charges of forgery and uttering. He was hanged on 16 November 1827 and apparently buried in his local churchyard at Skene, but in the early twentieth century his coffin was exhumed and found to contain only stones. The most likely reason is that grave robbers had taken his body, but a more romantic suggestion was that he had been cut down from the gallows alive and smuggled away to start a new life.

☆ FIRST bank robbery in Australia

Bank of Australia, George Street (now Dalley Street), Sydney.
Sunday 14 September 1828

Top London cracksman Sudden Solomon (real name George Blackston, aka Blaxton) realised that a drain cover in Lower George Street led to a tunnel that went right under the foundations of the Bank of Australia. For nearly three weeks he and four cronies dug a side tunnel until they estimated they were below the strongroom. Skinny Charlie Farrell squeezed through a hole in the floor and passed through £750 in English silver money, 2,000 sovereigns, £14,500 in banknotes and 2,030 Spanish dollars, which were then legal tender in Australia. Before they left they destroyed scores of ledgers, bills and receipts, thus wiping out the debts of many customers. Within a year Sudden Solomon, now broke, was caught trying to rob a gambling den. After serving eighteen months on Norfolk Island – 'a place of the extremest punishment short of death' – he offered to reveal all the details of the robbery for a pardon and free passage to England. The gang was quickly rounded up but while waiting for his passage to England Solomon ran out of money, attempted to rob a small shop, and ended up back in prison with his own gang members. He was found dead in a swamp in 1844.

☆ FIRST execution by William Calcraft

Thomas Lister and George Wingfield, Lincoln. Friday 27 March 1829

The scaffold baptism of William Calcraft, Britain's most famous executioner, was the hanging of not one but two criminals – Lister for burglary and Wingfield for highway robbery. After this first resounding success he remained Chief Hangman (officially 'Executioner for the City of London and Middlesex') for a record 45 years. A cobbler by trade, Calcraft became an executioner after hawking meat pies around Newgate for extra income. As a result of meeting hangman John Foxen (or Foxton) he began flogging juvenile offenders for ten shillings a week, and when Foxen died on 14 February 1829 Calcraft was appointed his successor. Sworn in on 4 April 1829, his wage was one guinea a week, with an extra guinea per capita for each execution and an allowance for cats-o'-nine-tails and birch rods. He supplemented his income by the sale of ropes and the belongings of his victims. Although Calcraft was the most famous hangman of the century, he seems to have been particularly incompetent – clumsy, bungling and notoriously unable to calculate the correct length of rope required for each individual hanging. This meant that most victims strangled rather than breaking their necks, and he frequently had to rush below the scaffold and pull on his victim's legs to hasten death.

☆ FIRST woman hanged by William Calcraft

Esther Hibner, London. Monday 13 April 1829

Esther Hibner, dubbed the 'Evil Monster', had been found guilty of the murder by starvation of her apprentice Frances Colppits. On the day of her execution she refused to dress, and the warders resorted to putting a black skirt over her nightgown. She had to be strait-jacketed to prevent her attacking the execution party, and it took two officers to manhandle her onto the scaffold. Unperturbed, Calcraft dispatched her with ease and the crowd roared, 'Three cheers for the hangman!'

☆ FIRST uniformed British statutory police force starts patrols

4 Whitehall Place, London. 18:00 Tuesday 29 September 1829

In September 1829, despite fears that the introduction of a police force was an infringement of civil liberties, the Metropolitan Police began patrolling the streets of London twelve hours a day, seven days a week. Nicknamed 'Peelers' and 'Bobbies' after their founder Sir Robert Peel, constables wore a blue uniform (to distinguish them from the military who wore red) with a top hat which doubled as a useful perch for looking over high walls. They also carried a rattle for attracting attention and a twenty-inch truncheon for protection. Police headquarters was in Whitehall Place but it was the name of the public entrance in Great Scotland Yard which became synonymous with the Met. In the first six months just over half the officers recruited were dismissed, mainly for drunkenness – indeed, the holders of Warrants Number 1 and 2, William Atkinson and William Alcock, were sacked on 29 and 30 September, the first and second day of patrols, for being drunk. The prime function of the new force was not the apprehension of criminals but crime prevention and in that their success was soon evident: in four years, loss from robberies was reduced from £1 million to £200,000. One social repercussion was that shopkeepers, previously reluctant to display their wares, began to introduce window displays.

✻ LAST person executed in for forgery England

Thomas Maynard, Old Bailey, London. Thursday 31 December 1829

The original punishment for forging title deeds was to be pilloried, have both ears sliced off, both nostrils slit open and seared, have all lands confiscated, and be imprisoned perpetually – but in 1634 forgery became a capital offence. It is thought that the first forger to be executed was John Carr, an Irish swindler who began forging seamen's wills; he was executed at Tyburn on 16 November 1750. Maynard was the last, having been tried at the Old Bailey on 10 September 1829 and convicted of 'uttering' (ie, passing forged notes into general circulation) and of forging Customs House Warrants to the value of £1,973.

✻ LAST person to be punished in the pillory in England

Peter James Bossy, Newgate, London. Tuesday 22 June 1830

In 1816 the pillory was abolished in England except for perjury and subornation (persuading someone to commit a crime). On 15 April 1830 at the Old Bailey, 31-year-old Bossy was found guilty of 'wilful and corrupt perjury' and sentenced to seven years' transportation, six months' imprisonment and to stand for one hour in the pillory, which he did at the Old Bailey on 22 June. Bossy was the last person to be so punished, and in 1837 the pillory was finally abolished altogether in England.

DID YOU KNOW?

The word pillory (*previous page*) comes from the Latin 'speculatorium', a place of observation or 'peep-hole'. Victims' heads and hands were held in three holes set in a hinged wooden frame, making the victim an easy target for any missile thrown by passers-by. The difference between the pillory and the stocks? The pillory traps head and hands while the stocks trap the feet.

☆ FIRST death of a Metropolitan Policeman on duty

PC Joseph Grantham, Smith's Place near Skinner Street, Somers Town, Euston. Tuesday 29 June 1830

Whilst patrolling a rough area known as Somers Town, PC Grantham spotted two drunk Irishmen quarrelling over a woman. It transpired the two men had started fighting after one of them had been beating his wife – Grantham intervened and was kicked to death by all three. A kick in the temple from young bricklayer Michael Duggan led to Grantham's death a few minutes later. However, the coroner's jury exonerated Duggan, claiming that Grantham had caused his own death by 'over-exertion in the discharge of his duty'. The day before he was murdered, Grantham's wife gave birth to twins.

☆ FIRST US bank robbery

Edward Smith, City Bank, Wall Street, New York City. March 1831

Though listed as robbery, Smith's crime was in fact burglary: using an ingenious duplicate key he removed $245,000 from City Bank, Wall Street, New York City and was caught after breaking the first rule of theft – 'Don't spend it all at once'. On 11 May 1831, after a short spectacular spending spree America's first bank robber (actually an English burglar) was sentenced to five years' hard labour in Sing Sing. Over $185,000 was recovered.

* LAST man gibbeted in Britain

James Cook, Aylestone, Leicestershire. Sunday 12 August 1832

Cook, a 21-year-old printer and bookbinder, owed twelve shillings to London engraver and tool cutter John Paas. On 30 May 1832 when Paas arrived at Cook's business premises in Leicester to collect, Cook beat him to death with an iron bar. Taking stiff drinks to fortify himself, Cook dismembered the body with a saw and a meat cleaver, then started cremating the pieces in the open grate of his fire. Leaving a few pieces to burn he made his drunken way home, not realising that the fat from the burning flesh was soaking into the wood chips and creating a giant candle. During the night the chimney caught fire, and neighbours who broke in to douse it found pieces of meat blazing in the fire. Summoned to the scene, Cook claimed that it was rotten horse meat that had been intended for his dog. He then returned home and made a run for it. The next morning, doctors examined the 'dog food' and announced that it was a human thigh bone and pelvis. Two police officers caught up with Cook as he was rowing out from Liverpool docks to board the *Carle of Calton*, bound for America. He jumped overboard and swam ashore from where, despite an attempt to poison himself with laudanum, he was returned to Leicester and tried. At 09:30 on 10 August 1832 he was hanged outside Leicester Prison in front of 30,000 people. After hanging for an hour his body was taken to the local infirmary where it was anatomised for medical students. Two days later Cook's corpse was dressed in the execution outfit and encased in an iron gibbet 33 feet above the junction of Aylestone Road and Saffron Lane, where a further 20,000 locals came to see the display. However, the crowd took no moral lesson from witnessing Cook's fate, and instead became so riotous and licentious that the authorities removed the body after only three days and buried it on the spot. In 1953, workmen digging a ditch discovered the coffin and irons, which were exhibited in Leicester's Guildhall and later at the National Prison Museum near Rugby. A replica set is still on show at the Guildhall, Leicester.

☆ FIRST private detective agency

Le Bureau des Renseignements, 12 rue Cloche-Perche, Paris. 1833

In 1833 Eugène François Vidocq, the world's first detective (*see 1811*), became the world's first professional private detective when he founded Le Bureau des Renseignments au Service des Intérêts Privés, the first known private detective agency. His services were available for an annual subscription of twenty francs, or for five francs per interview plus a percentage of any goods recovered. It was a successful enterprise, and at its peak Vidocq's agency was dealing with forty clients a day. He hired ex-convicts as agents, giving them such advice as 'The best way to tail someone without being seen is to walk in front of them,' and, 'In the underworld two and two do not make four. Two and two make twenty-two.' The police tried many times to shut down the agency. In 1842, after solving an embezzlement case, Vidocq was arrested on suspicion of unlawful imprisonment and taking money under false pretences. He was sentenced to five years and fined 3,000 francs but claimed that he had been framed by the authorities because his success was proving an embarrassment. Vidocq won his appeal but the police got the result they wanted because the bad publicity surrounding the case forced the closure of his business.

✳ LAST person in Scotland executed for rape

Mark Devlin, Town House, Dundee. Tuesday 20 January 1835

Twenty-six years old and 'rather good looking', Mark Devlin was condemned for the rape of thirteen-year-old Ann McLachlan behind the hill called 'The Law'. At 01:00 on the morning of his execution, Devlin was awoken by carpenters building the scaffold – he promptly went back to sleep.

☆ FIRST official plain clothes Detective Branch in Britain formed

Scotland Yard, London. Monday 15 August 1842

Six detectives combined to become Britain's first regularly constituted detective force, under the joint command of former Bow Street Runner Inspector Nicholas Pearce and his deputy Inspector John Haynes. *Punch* magazine satirised the members of the new Detective Branch as 'Defectives.' In 1877 The Detective Branch was dissolved and reformed as the CID (Criminal Investigation Department).

DID YOU KNOW?

The first detective novel was Wilkie Collins's *The Moonstone* whose hero Sergeant Cuff, the first fictional detective, was based on the pock-marked Detective Sergeant Jonathan Whicher of Scotland Yard's Detective Branch. Whicher, who never made a mistake, was known as 'the Prince of Detectives'.

* LAST person in England imprisoned for denying the existence of God

George Holyoake, Gloucester Assizes. Monday 15 August 1842

For many years social reformer Holyoake taught mathematics at the Mechanics' Institution in his native Birmingham. On 24 May 1842, in the course of a walk from Birmingham to Bristol, Holyoake lectured at the Mechanics' Institution in Cheltenham, Gloucestershire, and in reply to a question made a flippant reference to the deity. Arrested on a charge of blasphemy on 1 June, he was committed by the magistrates for trial at the Gloucester Assizes, and on declining to swear to his own recognisances he was refused bail. He was tried at the Gloucester Assizes on 15 August, and after defending himself in a nine-hour speech he was convicted and sentenced to six months' imprisonment. In 1851, in a pamphlet entitled *The History of the Last Trial by Jury for Atheism in England* Holyoake appealed to the attorney-general and the clergy for a bill legalising secular affirmations. No alteration was made in the law.

❑ ONLY woman hanged at Berrima prison

Lucretia Dunkley, Berrima Gaol, NSW. Sunday 22 October 1843

Before farmer Henry Dunkley disappeared, Lucretia, his wife of nine years, was heard to say: 'What a thing it is to lie down and rise with a man you hate.' On 14 September 1842 Lucretia told farm workers Henry had left early to watch the trial of a cattle thief named Birkshire at the Berrima Court House. The truth, though, was that the previous night he had been brutally axed to death by Lucretia's lover, farm hand Martin Beech. Beech hacked Dunkley three times about the head then ordered Lucretia to hold a chamber pot and collect the blood oozing from the body. They then wrapped the body in two rugs and buried it near a waterhole 300 yards from the house. Rumour of Dunkley's disappearance reached the local constable, who organised a search which uncovered Dunkley's body: a wound in the side of the neck had cut through the jugular vein, and the vertebrae and the face had been smashed in. Lucretia feigned hysterics but Beech confessed immediately. Ironically, the trial was held at Berrima Court House, where Beech abandoned all hope, saying: 'I only have one life to lose and I would soon die this minute as live any longer.'

DID YOU KNOW?

Berrima prison, largely built by convicts in irons, had a fearsome reputation. In the mid-nineteenth century prisoners spent the first nine months of their sentence in total silence, in solitary confinement cells measuring eight feet by five feet, some smaller. In 1877 a Royal Commission investigated allegations of cruelty by the prison authorities but the complaints were not upheld. Berrima Gaol, now an all-female low-medium security prison, is the oldest Gaol still in operation in Australia.

☆ FIRST criminal caught by telegraph

John Tawell, Jerusalem Coffee House, City of London. Thursday 2 January 1845

Apothecary John Tawell led a double life. Few people realised that the respectable 61-year-old Quaker was a convicted forger – or that he had a secret mistress half his age in Sarah Hadler, aka Mrs Hart, whom he supported, with his two illegitimate children, in a small cottage in Salt Hill, Slough. He explained his visits by claiming to be Sarah's father-in-law, and after one such visit on 1 January 1845 a neighbour, Mary Anne Ashley, heard a stifled scream and saw a man dressed in Quaker clothes leaving the cottage. Mrs Ashley discovered Sarah lying the floor writhing in agony but she died before help arrived. Realising the stranger had probably left by train the local vicar went straight to Slough Station where the stationmaster, using the latest innovation, transmitted the following telegraph to Paddington Station: 'A murder has just been committed at Salt Hill. The suspect was seen to take the train which left at 19:42. He is in the garb of a Kwaker.' The misspelling was deliberate since the telegraph code that time did not have a letter 'Q'. At Paddington, Tawell was spotted by railway policeman Constable Williams, who put a jacket over his uniform and followed Tawell by bus and then on foot to the Jerusalem Coffee House. From there Tawell walked across London Bridge to a lodging house in Scott's Yard. Being a railway policeman without authority of arrest, Williams reported Tawell, and when the Metropolitan Police arrested him in the Jerusalem Coffee House the following morning he said: 'You must be mistaken. My station in life places me above suspicion.' He was so convinced his social status as a Quaker and apothecary would see the case dismissed that he had his horse and carriage waiting outside the court. When it was shown that Sarah died of prussic acid poisoning, and a chemist from Bishopsgate identified Tawell as having purchased two drachms of prussic acid on two consecutive days prior to the murder, Tawell's defence counsel Mr Kelly ridiculously claimed Sarah had died from cyanide ingested as apple pips – and when it was revealed that cyanide can only be obtained by distilling the pips he was dubbed 'Apple Pip Kelly'. Tawell was publicly hanged at Aylesbury on 28 March, and the electro-magnetic telegraph used to make the historic capture was put on show for a shilling a look.

* LAST recorded duel between two Englishmen on English soil

Henry Hawkey & James Seton, Portsmouth. Tuesday 20 May 1845

Seton, a former captain in the 11th Hussars, fell in love with Hawkey's 24-year-old wife Isabella – 'eager, vivacious and gay... a good dancer, fond of boating and riding to hounds. It was only natural that she should attract the admiration of her husband's friends.' Hawkey, a lieutenant in the Royal Marines, was humiliated by Seton's public flirting with his wife, who appeared to be enjoying the attention. He challenged Seton to a duel but Seton declined and promptly shared the last dance with Isabella. Infuriated, Hawkey kicked Seton in the shin and declared, 'You are a blackguard and villain, Seton. You can either fight me or be horsewhipped down the Portsmouth High Street.' The duel was held at dusk on a scrap of coastal wasteland six miles west of Portsmouth. Fifteen paces apart, Seton missed and Hawkey's pistol, mistakenly kept half-cocked, failed to fire. At the second attempt Hawkey hit Seton in the stomach and immediately fled to France to avoid prosecution. Seton died ten days later from his wounds after a bungled operation.

☆ FIRST European judicially hanged in New Zealand

Joseph Burns, North Shore, Auckland. Saturday 17 June 1848

The first naval base in New Zealand was founded at Devonport, Auckland, in 1841. On 22 October 1847 the hut belonging to the officer in charge, Lt Robert Snow, caught fire, killing Snow and his family. A few months later a former naval shipwright, John Burns, slashed the throat of his common-law wife Margaret Reardon, who survived the attack. At his trial for assaulting Margaret, Burns confessed to the Snow murders but withdrew his confession   at the resulting trial. Margaret testified that Burns told her he intended to rob and kill Snow. She claimed that she had warned him not to but that he had nonetheless left the house and later returned declaring the deed had been done. Found guilty, he was taken to the execution site by boat sitting on his own coffin and hanged on the exact spot where he had murdered the Snow family. On the scaffold he asked the chaplain to speak his last words, in which he admonished Margaret: 'The causes that have led him to this sad end are indulgence in two sinful courses – his fondness for bad women, and his love of drinking...'

☆ **FIRST** US murderer executed on dental evidence
❑ **ONLY** Harvard Professor to be hanged

John Webster, Boston, Massachusetts. 09:30 Friday 30 August 1850

Dr George Parkman was an odd-looking 60-year-old with glittering false teeth and a lower jaw so prominent that he was nicknamed 'Chin'. A generous benefactor of Harvard University, he funded the Parkman Medical College, and the Parkman Professorship of Anatomy and Physiology was named in his honour. Parkman loaned over $400 to John Webster, 56-year-old Erving Professor of Chemistry and Mineralogy at Harvard, and Webster pledged his famous mineral collection as security. At 13:30 on 23 November 1849, after learning that Webster had also pledged his collection as collateral to another creditor, Parkman went to Webster's laboratory to demand repayment, and an angry exchange ended with Webster savagely attacking Parkman and crushing his skull with a piece of firewood. Webster then spent five days dismembering the body and cremating the pieces in the lab furnace. Janitor Ephraim Littlefield had witnessed an earlier confrontation between Webster and Parkman, and became suspicious after finding the laboratory door constantly bolted and the wall by the furnace always red-hot. He chiselled his way through the lab wall, and when he broke through he saw a human pelvis, male genitalia and two pieces of leg. Taken into custody, Webster attempted suicide by swallowing strychnine but admitted nothing. Further searches uncovered more body parts, and in the furnace police found splinters of skull along with what appeared to be false teeth partially fused into the cinders. The sensational trial rested on proving that the remains were Parkman's but no head or hands could be found, without which there was no positive identification. The prosecution's key witness was Dr Nathan C Keep, Parkman's family dentist of 24 years, who stated that Parkman's abnormally large lower jaw had made the fitting of his dentures memorably difficult. Keep demonstrated that five of the teeth found in the furnace precisely matched the wax cast from which they were made – and this unassailable dental evidence sent Webster to the gallows.

DID YOU KNOW?

In 1869, when Charles Dickens visited Boston and was asked which of the city's great landmarks he would most like to see, he replied, 'The room where Doctor Parkman was murdered.'

☆ FIRST woman executed in California

Juanita, Downieville, California. Saturday 5 July 1851

Juanita was a 23-year-old Mexican former prostitute who lived in a mining camp in Downieville, California. When she fell in love with a Mexican miner it seemed that she had left her former life behind – until 4 July 1851 when Jack Cannon, a previous client unaware of her new status, sought to procure her services. She locked herself inside her cabin but Cannon broke in, whereupon Juanita stabbed him to death. A travelling attorney who attempted to defend her was kicked out of town and the camp doctor, who declared her pregnant, was overruled by three local 'experts' who gave the doctor 24 hours to leave town. When Juanita was condemned to be hanged from the highest girder of a bridge outside Downieville a local newspaper commented: 'If a Mexican raised his hand against an Americano and killed him it was his death warrant.' As she stood on the bridge with the rope round her neck a local approached to push her off, but without waiting for the final indignity she smiled, said, 'Adios, senores,' and jumped.

DID YOU KNOW?

Arguments still rage as to whether the execution of Juanita (*above*) was legal. If not, then the dubious honour of being the first woman legally executed in California goes to another Juanita, aka Evelita Spinelli. (*See 21 November 1941*)

✳ LAST execution on Guernsey

John Charles Tapner, St Peter Port, Guernsey. 08:00 Friday 10 February 1854

Married with three children, Tapner led a double life. He had a second family (his sister-in-law/mistress and their son) who lodged in the home of 74-year-old Mme Elizabeth Saujon in the Guernsey village of Canichers. On 18 October 1853 Mme Saujon was attacked, hit over the head and left to die in her house which had been ransacked, robbed and left burning. The evidence against Tapner was circumstantial but the prosecution successfully claimed that he went to the house to buy furniture, that an argument erupted and that Tapner attacked the old lady, doused her body with white spirit and set fire to the house in an attempt to destroy any clues. After a sensational thirteen-day trial the jury unanimously found Tapner guilty and he was sentenced to death. Local resident Victor Hugo was incensed and wrote to the Home Secretary but neither this nor a petition with 600 local signatures was enough to alter the decision. Two hundred ticket-holders witnessed a botched hanging by an amateur volunteer executioner in the garden next to the prison in St Peter Port – Tapner's bindings were too loose and the drop space too narrow, and as the trap was opened Tapner freed his hands and clutched the sides. The hangman dashed down and grabbed Tapner's legs, desperately pulling to release his grip. Tapner screamed for fifteen minutes, and the white hood turned blood red before he finally died, an event which so shook the hangman that he sank into a depression and died within three months. Crime in Guernsey is rare. At the time of this execution with a population of 40,000, there were only three people in prison. According to the death cell chaplain, Tapner confessed that he had committed every sin except murder by the age of thirteen!

☆ FIRST 'Great Train Robbery'
☆ FIRST serious professional crime tackled by the Scotland Yard Detective Branch

The Pierce Gang, London Bridge-Folkestone-Boulogne-Paris Bullion Train. 20:30 Tuesday 15 May 1855

The first 'Great Train Robbery', originally known as 'The Great Bullion Robbery', was solved due to a lack of honour among thieves. It was planned by professional criminal Edward Agar and former railway ticket printer William Pierce, who recruited two 'inside men': James Burgess, a railway guard, and William Tester, a clerk who provided information on security and bullion transfers. Agar duplicated safe keys obtained by Tester and Pierce, while Tester altered the guards' rota to place Burgess on the 15 May bullion train. Agar and Pierce bought tickets and boarded the train carrying carpet bags full of lead, and when the train was under way Agar slipped into Burgess's van where one by one he opened the safes with the duplicated keys, knocked the iron clamps off the wooden strongboxes and replaced the gold with lead. After replacing the iron fastenings and resealing the safes, he and Pierce alighted at Dover and returned to London with £14,000 worth of gold. It appeared to be the perfect robbery – until August, when Agar started an affair with nineteen-year-old Emily Campbell. In revenge, her boyfriend/pimp, a gangster named William Humphries, framed Agar for forgery. Sentenced to transportation to Australia for life, Agar told his long-term mistress, barmaid Fanny Kay, that Pierce would provide for her and their son. But the destitute Fanny put two and two together, and when Pierce reneged on the deal she reported her suspicions. When police interviewed Agar, who was aboard a prison hulk awaiting deportation, he decided to punish the double-crossing Pierce by spilling the beans. From 10-12 January 1857 Pierce, Burgess and Tester were tried at the Old Bailey with Agar and Fanny Kay as prosecution witnesses. Burgess and Tester were sentenced to transportation for fourteen years but Pierce, convicted only of larceny, received just two years, 'the first, 12th and 24th month to be spent in solitary confinement'.

☆ FIRST accused murderer to escape punishment after pleading temporary insanity

Daniel Sickles, Washington, DC. Tuesday 26 April 1859

Sickles married Teresa Bagioli in 1853, when he was 35 and she 17, and four years later he became a Democrat Congressman. They moved to Washington, DC, where Sickles neglected Teresa for several lovers and she developed a relationship with 'the handsomest man in all Washington society', District Attorney

Phillip Barton Key (son of Francis Scott Key, author of *The Star-Spangled Banner*). Informed of Teresa's infidelity by poison pen letter, Sickles made Teresa write a full confession. The next day, Sunday 27 February 1859, Sickles saw Key in Lafayette Square. He yelled, 'Key you scoundrel! You have dishonoured my house! You must die,' and shot the defenceless cuckolder. Though wounded, Key struggled with Sickles who shot him again, then stood over his victim, reloaded and shot him a third time, at point-blank range. Sickles surrendered at Attorney General Jeremiah Black's house and confessed to the murder. He secured several leading politicians to defend him, including Edwin M Stanton, a future secretary of war, and the trial opened on 4 April with Stanton arguing that Teresa's infidelity had left Sickles temporarily insane with grief and therefore not responsible for his actions. For the first time in US history this defence succeeded – Sickles was acquitted and was even considered a public benefactor for rescuing other women from Key's beastly charms. Some time after the acquittal Sickles admitted, 'Of course I intended to kill him. He deserved it.'

* LAST American pirate to be executed by hanging

Albert E Hicks, Bedloe's Island, New York. Friday 13 July 1860

Hicks was a notorious thug and freelance killer who ruled New York's waterfront, where even the organised gangs steered clear of him. Unfortunately one Captain Burr didn't recognise Hicks, and shanghaied him after putting laudanum in his rum. When Hicks awoke aboard the sloop *E A Johnson* he attacked Burr and two crewmen, decapitating two of them and chopping the fingers off a third as he clutched the ship's rail in a vain attempt to avoid being thrown overboard. After flashing his new-found wealth Hicks was arrested, tried for piracy and incarcerated in the Tombs Prison, where his notoriety attracted huge numbers of sightseers.

The great showman P T Barnum paid $25 and two boxes of cigars for a bust of his head, and traded a new suit of clothes with Hicks for his prison-worn suit. Later, Hicks complained that Barnum had swindled him with a suit that was inferior to his original outfit. A crowd of 10,000, many aboard specially chartered boats off shore, watched Hicks being led to the gallows, still complaining that the suit was a bad fit. After the hanging his body was buried in Calvary Cemetery from where it was stolen and sold to medical students who wanted to study the brain of such a notorious killer.

✳ LAST woman executed in Tasmania

Margaret Coghlin (aka Coghlan and Coughlin), Campbell Street Gaol, Hobart, Tasmania. Tuesday 18 February 1862

Margaret and John Coghlin, an elderly couple who ran a lodging house in Hobart, were both known for their heavy drinking and 'dissipated habits'. At 03:30 on Monday 6 January 1862 Margaret, who claimed John had locked her out of the house, shouted to the constable on duty, 'Oh Lord! Bless me, he's come home and cut his throat.' Constable Waller found John lying in bed with his throat cut and a razor in his left hand. The body was examined by a Dr Cairns, who discovered head wounds. Cairns concluded that the head injuries were the cause of death, that the throat wound had been inflicted afterwards, and that the head injuries could not have been self-inflicted. Margaret was arrested and as she was removed from the house she said: 'They have taken away the innocent one this time.' At the inquest Margaret admitted murdering her husband and making it look like suicide but when she appeared in the Supreme Court on 25 January she changed her story again and pleaded 'Not Guilty'. The jury took just ten minutes to find her guilty and she was sentenced to death, with her body going for dissection. She spent her last days dreading the execution, and to prevent her final suffering her eyes were bandaged before she left the death cell so she would not see the scaffold. She was supported all the way to the gallows praying continuously until the final drop. She left behind a confession blaming 'strong drink' for the murder.

❏ ONLY American executed for slave trading

Nathaniel Gordon, New York City. 14:30 Friday 21 February 1862

Nathaniel Gordon was the only US slave trader to be tried, convicted and executed 'for being engaged in the Slave Trade' in accordance with the Piracy Law of 1820. On 7 August 1860, his fourth run, Gordon loaded 897 slaves aboard his slave ship *Erie* at Sharks Point on the River Congo, intending to sell them in Cuba. A day later Erie was intercepted by the warship USS *Mohican* and captured as a pirate vessel in international waters, and on 9 November 1861 Gordon was convicted. The evening before his execution he attempted suicide with strychnine smuggled into his cell in a box of cigars. Thoughtfully, to give him time to recover, the authorities postponed his hanging, at the Tombs Prison, from noon until 14:30.

✳ LAST woman publicly executed in Scotland

Mary Reid (or Timney), Dumfries, Scotland. Tuesday 29 April 1862

On 13 January 1862 Timney had a bitter argument with her neighbour, forty-year-old spinster Ann Hannah, and bludgeoned her to death with a cloth beetle (a heavy mallet used to pound cloth). For twenty minutes prior to the hanging the mob assembled outside the jail could clearly hear Timney wailing in her cell. She continued wailing as she mounted the scaffold, crying, 'Oh, my puir weans! My weans! My puir weans!' Then, just as hangman William Calcraft was about to release the bolt, a letter arrived. Thinking it was a reprieve the officials stopped the execution to read the contents. It turned out to be a letter from the editor of a London paper requesting a full report of the execution as soon as possible – Calcraft immediately sent her to eternity, and as he did so the crowd heard one last scream. Timney was interred inside the prison walls.

✳ LAST man in Britain to commit suicide on the morning of his execution

Walker Moore, Lancaster Castle. 07:10 Saturday 30 August 1862

On 5 April 1862, a 37-year-old tailor named Walker Moore murdered his estranged wife Betty, 32, in a jealous rage at the Hare and Hounds public house in Lancashire. At 09:00, while Betty was on her knees cleaning the fire irons, he attacked her from behind and slashed her throat with a razor, later kissing her corpse and saying, 'She was a grand one.' Sentenced to death, he claimed there was no rope in existence that would hang him. On the final morning, with the crowds gathering outside to witness the hanging, he was taken to the Chapel yard for his regular 07:00 exercise. After ten minutes he was granted permission to use the toilet, as was his usual practice. The three water closets in the yard were all fed from a 5 x 15 foot lead tank holding about four feet of water – by the time the warders realised there was something amiss Moore had hauled himself into the cistern, tied a handkerchief round his neck, forced himself into an inescapable position beneath the water line and drowned. Police feared rioting among the would-be spectators outside, who became very vocal at being robbed of their entertainment!

✳ LAST woman publicly hanged at Newgate Prison

Catherine Wilson, Newgate, London. Monday 20 October 1862

Employers and husbands died suddenly around Catherine Wilson until she was finally arrested and convicted of poisoning. Her first husband died in mysterious circumstances; Captain Peter Mawer, who employed her as a housekeeper, died soon after promising that he had left her something in his will; and her next employer, Mrs Soames, died after Wilson had borrowed £9. Her next intended victim was Sarah Carnell, whom Wilson nursed with sulphuric acid. Wilson was arrested for attempted murder but acquitted after her lawyer convinced the jury the pharmacist must have made a mistake in labelling medicine bottles. Eventually the past caught up with her and she was sentenced to death for the murder of Mrs Soames. Some 20,000 people turned out to watch the hanging.

☆ FIRST armed bank robbery in the US

Edward Green, Malden, Massachusetts. Tuesday 15 December 1863

To distract him from his heavy debts 32-year-old postmaster Green started drinking excessively. On 15 December 1863 he went next door to the local bank to change a $20 bill. Noticing the only person on duty was the bank president's seventeen year-old son Frank Converse, Green went home, fetched his gun, and, finding Converse still alone, shot him point-blank in the forehead before helping himself to $5,000. No one suspected that the culprit might be working next door but after a month people noticed that Green had suddenly begun paying off his debts; when police questioned him he immediately broke down and confessed. On 13 April 1866, in Middlesex County Jail, America's first armed bank robber became America's first armed bank robber to be hanged.

☆ **FIRST** murder to be committed on a train in the United Kingdom

☆ **FIRST** transatlantic chase of a fugitive by a Scotland Yard detective

☆ **FIRST** US extradition case dealt with by Scotland Yard

Franz Muller, East End of London (between Bow and Wick). Saturday 9 July 1864

German-born tailor Franz Muller, 25, attacked 70-year-old bank clerk Thomas Briggs on a train between Bow and Hackney Wick, robbing him of his gold watch and throwing his victim out of the carriage. Briggs died without regaining consciousness shortly after he was found. Muller panicked and mistakenly took Briggs's hat, leaving his own custom-made original behind. The hat led police to name their suspect as Franz Muller but unfortunately Muller had already embarked on the SS *Victoria* for New York. Detective Tanner boarded a faster vessel, the *City of Manchester*, and was waiting to arrest him as he stepped ashore carrying Briggs' missing watch and hat. He was extradited, convicted, and publicly hanged outside Newgate Prison on 14 November 1864. To allay public fears regarding safety aboard trains the railway companies began to cut peep-holes between compartments. Quickly nicknamed 'Muller's Lights', they were eventually abandoned because men lost their privacy and women were afraid of Peeping Toms.

DID YOU KNOW?

The custom-made hat which led police to Muller was made by cutting down the crown of a top hat – for years afterwards squat top hats became the height of fashion and were known as 'Mullers'.

☆ FIRST organised daylight bank robbery in America

The James Gang, Liberty, Missouri. (Jesse and Frank James, Cole and Jim Younger, Arch Clements, Bud Pearce, George Shepherd, Payton Jones and Andy Mcguire) 14:00 Tuesday 13 February 1866

Using what would become their standard modus operandi, two of of the gang entered the Clay County Savings Association building and asked for change for a $10 bill. A third stationed himself just inside the door, a fourth just outside, and the others patrolled the street, one taking charge of the horses. The first robber drew a revolver, threatened to shoot cashier William Bird if he made any noise, and demanded all the money in the bank. But Bird was too scared to move, so they smacked him on the back of the head with the revolver and told him, 'Damn you, be quick!' After collecting the money the gang locked Bird and the bank manager (Bird's father, Greenup Bird) in the vault and then fled with $60,000 of loot – officially $5,008.46 in coin, $8,668 in greenbacks, $3,096 in state military bonds, $300 in old Farmer's Bank notes and $40,000 in US bonds, which proved useless, being non-negotiable. As they rode away down Franklin Street the gang 'hurrahed' the town, shooting indiscriminately and killing an innocent bystander, nineteen year-old student George Wymore. A posse pursued the gang but gave up after a sudden snowstorm obliterated all tracks. The James Gang went on to commit roughly one robbery a year for some fifteen years, netting an estimated $350,000.

DID YOU KNOW?

There was an earlier bank robbery on 18 October 1864 but this is regarded as a military operation by a group of 22 Confederate soldiers who robbed three banks in St Albans, Vermont, then fled to Canada where fourteen of them were arrested.

✳ LAST British convicts arrive in Australia

Fremantle. 10 January 1868

The last shipment comprised 451 prisoners including 60 Fenian agitators. In 80 years approximately 162,00 prisoners were transported, *c.*137,000 men and *c.*25,000 women

✳ LAST woman publicly hanged in Britain

Frances Kidder, Maidstone Prison. 12:00 Thursday 2 April 1868

Frances, 25, was married to huckster William Kidder. She deeply resented William's daughter Louisa (from a previous relationship) and consistently abused her, even threatening to kill her. On 25 August 1867 Frances drowned Louisa in a ditch: she must have held the struggling 11-year-old under as the water was only just over twelve inches deep. When Louisa's body was found, Frances claimed that they had fallen into the ditch together after being frightened by passing horses. This excuse was rightly rejected by the jury after just twelve minutes – in the condemned cell Frances confessed the murder to the prison chaplain. She frequently became hysterical while awaiting her execution, and when the day came she had to be helped onto the gallows and held on the trapdoors by two warders. She prayed intently while executioner William Calcraft strapped her wrists in front of her and put two leather straps around her body: one pinning her arms at elbow level and another around her legs to hold her long skirt down. He placed a white cotton hood over her head and adjusted the noose. Then he released the trap and some 2,000 people watched Frances drop three feet and struggle hard for two or three minutes. William Kidder reputedly stood in the crowd and watched his wife hang.

✳ LAST public execution in Scotland

Robert Smith, Dumfries Gaol, Dumfriesshire. Tuesday 12 May 1868

On 1 February 1868 Smith, a nineteen-year-old labourer, ravished, murdered and robbed nine-year-old Thomasina Scott in a wood near Annan – she had been on her way to buy family provisions and had 9s 11d in her purse. Afterwards Smith calmly walked into the town and bought tobacco before breaking into a cottage near Cummertrees where he shot Jane Crichton before stabbing and finally attempting to strangle her. Crichton's screams attracted the attention of two local boys and Smith ran off, returning to his lodgings in Dumfries where he was arrested a couple of days later. In April 'The Cummertrees Murderer' was convicted, the court reporter commenting, 'his face indicates susceptibility to fits of extreme passion, it is not of the low criminal type'. Five hundred people turned up to witness the execution but saw little as they were held behind barricades well away from the action. Just as Smith was to be dropped, the hangman, Thomas Askern, dissatisfied with the noose placement, halted proceedings, rearranged the rope, then pulled the bolt. Smith's death mask is on display in the Dumfries Museum & Camera Obscura.

✳ LAST person publicly hanged in Great Britain

Michael Barrett, Newgate Prison. 08:00 Tuesday 26 May 1868

At 15:45 on 13 December 1867 Irish rebel Michael Barrett led an attempt to free two Fenian prisoners from London's Clerkenwell House of Detention. The conspirators parked a wagon loaded with a large barrel of dynamite beside the prison wall and blew it up, which had the desired effect of bringing down the wall but also devastated the block of houses opposite – the tenements were 'stripped clearly of their frontages, left open like doll's houses with the kettles still on the hobs'. Six people were killed outright, six died later and 120 were injured, and because it was early afternoon nearly all the victims were women and children. Informers led police to arrest Barrett along with four men and a woman. At their trial two of the men turned queen's evidence against Barrett, demanding the reward for doing so. Barrett made a famously eloquent speech proclaiming his innocence but to no avail. On the day of his execution Barrett was led out of Newgate Prison wearing a short red jacket and grey striped trousers, his face 'white as marble'. His arrival was greeted with a mixture of cheers and hisses but he seemed oblivious, attentive only to what the priest was saying to him. His dignity impressed the crowd and when someone shouted 'Hats off!' everyone obeyed. Barrett's last words were spoken from under the hood, asking hangman William Calcraft to adjust the position of the rope. Calcraft obliged and instantly drew the bolt. The drop fell with a loud boom accompanied by a great cry from the crowd, 'neither an exclamation nor a scream.' Barrett died instantly, without a struggle. The composure with which Barrett met his end aroused admiration from many people and at 09:00 when Calcraft came to cut him down there were calls of 'Come on, body-snatcher! Take away the man you've killed.' Thus Calcraft performed the last public executions in England and Scotland and, three months later, the first private execution in England. (*See also last public hanging in the British Isles, 1875*)

DID YOU KNOW?

One of the saddest victims of the Clerkenwell bombing was Arthur Abbott who was blinded as a result of his injuries. He became a famous London figure, tramping through the streets carrying a notice recalling the outrage so no one would forget.

☆ FIRST private execution in Great Britain

Thomas Wells, Maidstone Prison. 10:30 Thursday 13 August 1868

On the 29 May 1868 Parliament passed the Capital Punishment within Prisons Bill, ending public hangings and directing that all future executions take place privately within prisons. The first person to be executed under the new law was eighteen-year-old railway carriage cleaner Thomas Wells. Wells's boss, stationmaster Edward Walshe, had caught Wells shooting at birds and given him an ultimatum: either make a full apology and promise never to repeat his actions or be dismissed. Wells declined to make an apology – instead he shot Walshe in the head. Rejecting his defence of insanity brought on by injuries sustained when he was almost crushed by a train, the jury took just five minutes to convict. Despite being a 'private' execution, it was attended by guests of the sheriff and sixteen journalists. Wells, wearing his railway porter's uniform with a flower in his buttonhole, was twice given stimulants to prevent him fainting but still collapsed while being pinioned. Like so many of Calcraft's victims, Wells died a slow and painful death lasting three or four minutes. The execution of Wells marked a trio of firsts and lasts for Calcraft, who also executed the last person publicly hanged in England and the last in Scotland.

☆ FIRST private execution of a woman in Great Britain

Priscilla Biggadike, Lincoln. 09:00 Monday 28 December 1868

Priscilla and Richard Biggadike lived in the village of Stickney, Lincolnshire, with their three children and two lodgers: rat-catcher Thomas Proctor and fisherman George Ironmonger. On the evening of 30 September 1868 Richard Biggadike ate tea of hot cakes and mutton but within minutes was in agony, vomiting violently, saying 'I can't live long in this state.' The local doctor diagnosed food poisoning, at which Priscilla produced the cake he had been eating to prove it was harmless. Biggadike died at 06:00 the following morning and the autopsy revealed substantial traces of arsenic. Priscilla was arrested and told police that she had found a suicide note in her husband's pocket, adding that someone else must have written it since he couldn't write – but when asked to produce the note she claimed to have burnt it. Ten days later she changed her story, saying she had seen Proctor (who may well have been her lover and father of her third child) putting white powder into her husband's tea. She was nonetheless found guilty and sentenced to hang. When the 29-year-old stepped onto the scaffold she continued to proclaim her innocence, saying: 'All my troubles are over. Shame, you're going to hang me. Surely my troubles are over.' Unfortunately her troubles weren't quite over because the executioner, the notoriously clumsy Thomas Askern, positioned the noose incorrectly which meant that Priscilla struggled for several agonising minutes. In 1882, on his deathbed, Thomas Proctor confessed to putting the arsenic in the tea.

☆ FIRST assassination in Canada
✳ LAST public hanging in Canada

Patrick James Whelan, Ottawa, Canada. Thursday 11 February 1869

Canada's first murder after achieving Dominion status was the assassination of the Hon. Thomas D'Arcy McGee, one of the founding members of Canada's first independent government. At the age of 23 McGee, the leader of the 'Young Ireland' underground rebellion, was forced to flee his homeland with a price of 300 guineas on his head. He emigrated to Canada in 1857 and after being elected to the Legislative Assembly he dropped his support for the Fenian cause, stating that the use of violence was counter-productive. The Fenians denounced him as a traitor, and he was assassinated at 02:15 on 7 April 1868 as he returned home after a late-night sitting of the Canadian House of Commons. As he put the key in the front door of his house in Ottawa, Irish tailor Patrick James Whelan shot him in the back of the neck, the bullet passing through the upper part of his throat and out through his mouth. Arrested within 24 hours, Whelan fiercely denied being the assassin but the evidence was overwhelming. When the jury announced him guilty Whelan said, 'Now I am held to be a black assassin. And my blood runs cold. But I am innocent. I never took that man's blood.' His execution at 11:00 on Thursday 11 February 1869 – Canada's last public hanging – was watched by a crowd of 5,000 people. Whelan's last words were 'God save Ireland and God save my soul.'

❑ ONLY murderer hanged in a policeman's uniform

Michael Flanigan, Melbourne, Australia. Wednesday 31 March 1869

Flanigan, an Irish policeman, emigrated to Australia in 1859 and joined the Victoria Police Force two years later. Stationed in Victoria's western districts he was persistently charged with drunkenness, losing his horse, dishonesty and gambling whilst on duty. Flanigan was transferred to Hamilton but continued to break the rules until eventually he was dismissed and instructed to clean and return his accoutrements. It fell to Station Sergeant Thomas Hull to inspect Flanigan's equipment and issue a receipt for its return. On inspection Hull harshly reprimanded Flanigan for the condition of his sidearm and told him to clean it again. As Hull left the room Flanigan fired a number of shots at his back, mortally wounding him. For his execution, having been granted special permission to do so, 36-year-old Flanigan strode boldly onto the gallows at Melbourne Jail wearing his police uniform.

☆ FIRST private execution in Dublin

Andrew Carr, Richmond (later Mountjoy) Prison, Dublin. Thursday 28 July 1870

Carr, an army pensioner, slashed the throat of his lover in revenge for a previous snub. The doctor recommended an eight foot drop but the black-masked hangman insisted on giving Carr an extraordinary drop of fourteen feet – probably the longest in judicial hanging records. So Carr wasn't hanged: he was decapitated by the fall, an execution so gruesome that one local newspaper suggested that had the hanging been public it would have been the last in Dublin.

❑ ONLY US President to have personally hanged criminals

Grover Cleveland. Erie County, New York. Friday 6 September 1872 and Friday 14 February 1873

While he was sheriff of Erie County, New York State, future president Grover Cleveland hanged two murderers: Patrick Morrissey, who had been condemned for stabbing his mother to death, and Jack Gaffney, a gambler who shot and killed a man during a card game in Buffalo. At Morrissey's execution on 6 September 1872 one of Cleveland's deputies reportedly took a slug of brandy and offered to spring the trap that would send Morrissey to his death, but Cleveland replied: 'No, I have to do it myself. I am the sheriff and it is part of the sheriff's duties.' Cleveland sprung the trap at 12:05 and Morrissey was pronounced dead at 12:14. As 22nd and 24th president of the USA, Cleveland is also the only president to have been re-elected following a defeat and thereby serve separate, rather than concurrent, terms.

❏ ONLY woman in South Australia to go to the gallows

Elizabeth Woolcock, Adelaide Gaol, South Australia. 08:00 Tuesday 30 December 1873

At her trial for murdering her husband Thomas, 25-year-old Elizabeth Woolcock said that she had only married him 'to spite those who were opposed to the marriage'. Reputedly she was a victim of domestic violence and, having considered hanging herself, sent her ten-year-old stepson John to buy threepenn'orth of white precipitate powder with which to poison Thomas. A month after she had begun putting the powder in Thomas's food the mercury took effect; Thomas died on 4 August 1873. Despite the jury's recommendation for mercy on account of her youth, Elizabeth was condemned to hang. Calm and collected, she mounted the scaffold in a plain white dress, holding a bunch of flowers. When the bolt was drawn she dropped several feet and appeared to struggle for some minutes, but it was found that the neck was dislocated. For many years afterwards the area where she lived was known as 'poison flats'.

✳ LAST hanging by William Calcraft in London

James Godwin, Newgate Prison, London. Monday 25 May 1874

On 22 April 1874 rug-maker John Godwin, 27, battered his wife Louisa to death with a piece of wood, thus earning the dubious distinction of being the last Newgate victim of hangman William Calcraft. Even after 45 years' experience Calcraft was incapable of judging the length of rope required, so his victims died a slow, painful death. *The Times* reported: 'Godwin died hard; his breast heaved convulsively, his hands were raised repeatedly to his throat. And these convulsions continued, not ceasing until some minutes had past.' Calcraft was willing to continue as an executioner but, being 70, he was compelled to retire on a City of London pension of one guinea a week. Most reference works cite this as Calcraft's last hanging but there was in fact one more. (*See 10 August 1874*)

☆ FIRST woman hanged for murdering her grandchild
☆ FIRST woman executed inside Newgate Prison

Frances Stewart, Newgate Prison. Monday 29 June 1874

Stewart, a 48-year-old widow, lived in Chelsea with her daughter Carrie, Carrie's hard-drinking husband Joseph Scriverner, and their 12-month-old son Ernest. The constant rowing between mother- and son-in-law came to a head in 1874 when, Carrie having asked her to leave, Mrs Stewart stormed out of the house taking the baby with her. Two days later a letter arrived saying, 'Dear Carrie, Come at once as I've done a murder and I want you to give me in charge of the police. I've killed the dear boy. From Frances Stewart.' She also wrote to Joseph, telling him that it was all his fault and saying: 'it is the only thing I can do to make your heart ache as you have made mine.' Ernest's body was recovered on the bank of the River Thames near Albert Bridge. Frances claimed he had accidentally fallen in from Albert Bridge but offered no reason as to why she hadn't tried to rescue him. She was executed by William Marwood, who gave her the extraordinarily short drop of less than three feet.

✳ LAST execution by William Calcraft

John MacDonald, Exeter, Devon. Monday 10 August 1874

It has always been thought that Calcraft's last hanging was that of John Godwin on 25 May 1874 (*see above*). However, recent brilliant detective work by English execution-historian Matthew Spicer has uncovered a later Calcraft execution. It would appear that after being pensioned off as hangman by the City of London, he accepted an offer to hang ex-Marine John MacDonald, who battered his unfaithful mistress Bridget Walsh to death with a bedpost in Plymouth, Devon, on 30 June 1874. MacDonald immediately attempted suicide by taking acetate poison and then cutting his own throat, and having survived that attempt he tried to starve himself to death in prison. In his will (written just prior to his hanging) he bequeathed £11 to pay for Bridget's funeral. With this execution ended Calcraft's record 45-year career as hangman, which included the last public and first private hangings in England. Once an amiable man who took delight in breeding rabbits, his career left him surly and sinister-looking: with long hair and beard and a slouching gait, he habitually wore scruffy black clothes, a fob chain and a tall hat. He died at Poole Street, Hoxton, London, on 13 December 1879.

✳ LAST public execution in the British Isles

Joseph Philippe Le Brun, St Helier, Jersey, Channel Islands. Thursday 12 August 1875

Jersey police claimed that on 15 December 1874 Le Brun, 52, shot dead his sister Nancy and seriously wounded her husband Philippe Laurens. Le Brun protested his innocence and at his trial he denied both charges, saying he had no motive. The prosecution could prove no more than the fact that Le Brun was in the locality, and implied that the incident was the result of a family quarrel but the jury nonetheless found him guilty. The day before the execution Laurens visited his brother-in-law in the death cell and told him, 'I did not come here to argue with you. I forgive you, but I say that you committed the crime. Adieu!' The Parliamentary order prohibiting public executions in England had not yet been registered in Jersey, and the next day the scaffold was surrounded by 84 halberdiers, with another 100 posted in adjacent streets to control the huge crowd, which watched Le Brun drop through the trap and heard the priest cry, 'He's innocent! He's innocent!' (*See also last public hanging in Great Britain, 1868*)

DID YOU KNOW?

Although this was the last public execution in the British Isles, the last in Great Britain took place seven years earlier (*see 1868*). This nicety arises because Great Britain comprises England, Scotland and Wales but does not include the Crown Dependencies of the Channel Islands or the Isle of Man. (The United Kingdom is different again, comprising Great Britain and Northern Ireland.)

☆ FIRST stage coach robbery by the legendary Black Bart (Charles Boles)
✳ LAST stage coach robbery by Black Bart

Black Bart, Calaveras County, California. Monday 26 July 1875 and Wednesday 3 November 1883

The coach, driven by John Shine, was held up at Funk Hill on the Sonora to Milon Road, four miles east of Copperopolis. Black Bart, wearing a mask made from a linen duster and a flour sack, jumped out in front of the coaches, levelled a shotgun at Shine and politely requested, 'Please throw down the box,' – adding, less politely, 'If he dares to shoot, give him a volley boys.' It was then that Shine noticed half a dozen rifles poking out of the brush. Bart took $60 in gold notes from the Wells Fargo express box and an undetermined amount from the US Mail pouch. Shine drove off but soon returned to the scene to find that the six rifle barrels were just blackened sticks of wood. For eight years the mysterious and polite Black Bart plagued Wells Fargo coaches using an unloaded shotgun, always on foot, and making a point of never robbing either the driver or passengers of their personal money. Between robberies he lived the high life as Charles Bolton, mine-owner and San Francisco dandy. After his fourth robbery Black Bart left this doggerel:

> I've labored long and hard for bread
> For honor and for riches
> But on my corns too long you've tread
> You fine-haired sons of bitches.

Thereafter he left equally bad poems after each robbery. His 29th and last robbery, on 3 November 1883, was at exactly the same place as his first but did not meet with the same success: he was wounded and later captured. On 16 November 1883 he was sentenced to six years in San Quentin Prison and 'seemed rather pleased with the sentence'. He became a model prisoner and was released in January 1888.

☆ FIRST recorded official use of dogs by police to capture a murderer

William Fish, 3 Moss Street, Blackburn. Sunday 16 April 1876

On 28 March 1876 seven-year-old Emily Holland went missing from Birley Street, Blackburn, after telling a witness that she was 'going to fetch half an ounce of tobacco for a man in the street'. The next morning a child's naked torso was found in a nearby Bastwell Field wrapped in two bloodstained copies of the *Preston Herald* – minus head, arms and legs. That afternoon a child's legs were discovered stuffed in a drain a few miles away in Lower Cunliffe, also wrapped in two copies of the *Preston Herald*. A post mortem revealed the child had been sexually assaulted, bled to death from having her throat cut, and then been dismembered.

The post mortem also noted that the trunk had several different people's hair clippings stuck to it and so two local barbers came under suspicion, one of whom, William Fish, kept old newspapers. Fish was co-operative and allowed police to search his home three times. The third search revealed that four issues of the *Preston Herald*, corresponding with those used to wrap the torso and legs, were missing from his date-ordered stack of papers but Fish claimed he had used them to light the fire and there was insufficient evidence to charge him. Then Chief Constable Potts received an extraordinary offer from a painter named Peter Taylor, who owned a springer spaniel and a half-breed bloodhound named Morgan, which he claimed could find Emily's missing remains. On 16 April the dogs searched Bastwell and Lower Cunliffe but found nothing. Then they were taken to Fish's home, where Morgan started barking in front of the bedroom fireplace. In a small recess in the chimney was a parcel containing fragments of human skull, hands and forearms, wrapped in a bloodstained copy of the *Manchester Courier*. Fish was hanged at Kirkdale Gaol, Liverpool, on Monday 14 August 1876, while Potts was ridiculed for his historic decision to allow dogs to do police work. A popular riddle of the day ran: 'When was Mr Potts like the beggar Lazarus?' Answer: 'When he was licked by dogs.'

✻ LAST woman executed by decapitation in Japan

O-Den Takahashi, Yokohama, Japan. Friday 31 January 1879

Takahashi was a prostitute who slit the throat of a sleeping customer with a straight razor to rob him of a paltry 26 yen. Her decapitation was botched twice. On the first attempt the razor-sharp blade merely sliced the back of her head, leaving her rolling around in her own blood calling out the name of her lover. The second attempt also failed, and the execution finally ended with the executioner hacking his way through her neck 'like cutting a daikon' ('giant radish') while she was still conscious. Her sexual organs were removed and later put on display.

☆ FIRST portrait of a wanted fugitive published in a British newspaper

Percy Mapleton (aka Lefroy), Daily Telegraph. *Friday 1 July 1881*

On 27 June 1881, 64-year-old coin dealer Isaac Gold was brutally murdered on the 14:00 London to Brighton express train. At Preston Park station the ticket collector noticed a man smothered with blood who, on inquiry, claimed he had been attacked by two passengers who had fled. There was no evidence against the man, Percy Mapleton, but he was arrested because police thought he might have attempted suicide (then a criminal offence). A detective escorted him to his home in Surrey and waited patiently outside while Mapleton went in to change his clothes. Meanwhile Gold's body had been found beside the railway track, stabbed in the chest and shot in the neck. Police rushed into the house only to find that Mapleton had escaped through the back door. On 1 July, at the request of the police, the *Daily Telegraph* made history by publishing an artist's impression of Mapleton with the unflattering description: 'Age 22. Middle height, very thin, sickly appearance... low felt hat, black coat, teeth much discoloured... very round shouldered... forehead and chin are both receding... jawbones are prominent, his cheeks sunken and shallow... upper lip is thin and drawn inwards... His eyes are grey and large'. The response led to several arrests including one innocent suspect who was charged with the murder. Then on 8 July, after a tip-off from the landlady of Mapleton's new lodging in Stepney, he was arrested – Mrs Bickers claimed the £200 reward despite not having seen the picture in the *Daily Telegraph*. Reporting on the trial, *The Times* newspaper noted that their competitor's picture 'did not bear any resemblance to the prisoner'. At 08:59 on 29 November 1881 at Lewes Gaol Mapleton was hanged 'without a struggle'. His last words were to the hangman William Marwood; he said 'Do you think the rope will break?'

☆ FIRST use of whistles by Metropolitan Police

London. February 1886

Whistles replaced rattles after experiments showed while rattles could be heard clearly over 400 yards and indistinctly over another 300 yards, whistles were clearly audible for 900 yards.

✳ LAST woman hanged in New York State

Roxalana Druse, Herkimer, NY. 12:00 Monday 28 February 1887

Roxalana lived in a frontier cabin in Little Falls, New York, with her two children and her husband John. When she was 40 Roxalana and her retarded daughter, Mary, beat 72-year-old John to death, chopped up his body and boiled down the remains. They were caught because Roxalana's twelve-year-old son informed the police that his father was missing. At her trial Roxalana alleged that she had killed John because he worked her too hard – Mary was given a prison sentence and Roxalana condemned to death. At her execution, rather than being dropped through a trap door she was jerked upwards by a weighted rope. This technique, known as the 'twitch-up method', failed to break her neck and she took fifteen agonising minutes to strangle to death on the noose. The scene so upset the officials that it was decided to abandon hanging as the method of execution and replace it with the electric chair, which was inaugurated in 1890 (*See 6 August 1890*).

❑ ONLY woman hanged in Queensland

Ellen Thompson, Boggo Road Jail, Brisbane, Queensland. Monday 13 June 1887

Ellen arrived in Australia from Cork, Ireland, in 1858 when she was eleven. During the Palmer River gold rush in the early 1870s she was known to be in Cooktown, widow of William Wood, and struggling to support her children. Arriving in Port Douglas about 1878 she began working as housekeeper to William Thompson on a farm on the Mossman River. Thompson was 24 years her senior but they married in November 1880 after the birth of a daughter, Helen. It was an unhappy union and grew increasingly violent. Ellen began an affair with a young Marine deserter named John Harrison, and when William Thompson was shot dead both Ellen and Harrison were sentenced to death. On the eve of execution Harrison admitted that he alone had killed Thomson, claiming self defence, but the confession was too late – they were both hanged. A post mortem phrenological examination found Ellen to be 'combative and destructive, with a powerful libido'.

❑ ONLY jail-breaker to become a judge

Sakigake Watanabe, Fukue Island, Japan. 1890

Sakigake Watanabe's downfall was a geisha – to keep her in the lavish lifestyle she expected he began embezzling money from his employers, for which, in 1880, he was sentenced to life with hard labour. After a failed escape attempt he was sent to the fearsome Miike coalmine where few survived their sentence but amazingly, two years later, he escaped after hiding in a toilet. His father, a low-ranking justice official, helped arrange a false identity after which Sakigake became a civil servant, a tax official and then a judicial clerk. By 1887 he had the chance to become an assistant judge but this meant he would have to move to Fukue, which came under the jurisdiction of Nagasaki, where he had been convicted. But the opportunity was too good to miss: he took the job, and three years later he became a full judge, hearing criminal cases. But on 19 February 1891 he was recognised by the prosecutor who had handled his embezzlement trial. At first Sakigake tried to bluff, claiming that he was his own younger brother, but after five days' interrogation he confessed. His father received eighteen months for forging identity papers, and 33-year-old Sakigake was returned to the coal mines. Luckily for him, public sympathy was on his side and he was pardoned late in 1892.

☆ FIRST execution using the electric chair

William Kemmler (aka John Hart), Auburn, New York. 06:51 Wednesday 6 August 1890

On 29 March 1889 Kemmler axed his mistress Tillie Zeiglar to death in a drunken fit of jealousy. The night before his execution he danced and sang to a banjo played by a fellow death-row inmate, but the following morning he begged Deputy Sheriff Joseph Veiling: 'I'll promise you that I won't make any trouble... Don't let them experiment on me more than they ought to.' Veiling shaved Kemmler's crown then cut the back of his trousers, exposing Kemmler's spine for the second electrode. Kemmler entered the death chamber wearing yellow-patterned prison trousers, a dark grey sack jacket with matching waistcoat, a white linen shirt, highly polished black shoes and a bow tie which he self-consciously straightened. At 06:34 Warden Durston asked if he had any last words and he said: 'Gentlemen, I wish you all good luck. I believe I'm going to a good place, and I'm ready to go. A great deal has been said about me that's untrue. I'm bad enough.

It's cruel to make me out worse.' Kemmler removed his jacket and sat in the chair but was asked to stand again because Durston suddenly realised he needed to cut another hole in the back of the shirt. Kemmler told him, 'Take your time Warden, and do it right. There's no rush. I don't want to take any chances on this thing you know.' When the electrodes were securely attached Durston said, 'God bless you Kemmler,' who replied 'Thank you.' Durston then said, 'Goodbye William' but there was no reply. Durston rapped twice on the door, the executioner threw the switch and Kemmler's torso convulsed. His face and hands turned first red then ashen – his staring eyes terrified the 25 witnesses. One of his fingers clenched so tight the nail cut into the flesh and blood started trickling down the arm of the chair. Fierce red spots appeared on his face. After seventeen seconds Edward Spitzka, a celebrated anatomist, announced, 'He's dead.' The electricity was turned off and the body sagged forward like a rag doll. But as Durston started to remove the headpiece Kemmler's chest heaved, a gurgling sound came from his throat and foam bubbled out of his mouth. The switch was thrown again and the lifeless body sat up taut as the current surged back though it. This time smoke rose from the top of his head and drops of blood sparkled on his face, accompanied by a sizzling sound like meat frying in a pan; the smell of charred skin, singed hair, urine and faeces pervaded the room. At 06:51 Spitzka signalled Durston to turn the power off. Kemmler's second electrocution had lasted about a minute. Shocked witnesses agreed with Spitzka: 'I've never seen anything so awful. I believe this will be the first and last execution of the kind.' Though most of the press denounced electrocution as little more than torture, the *New York Times* said it would be absurd to go back to 'the barbarism of hanging'. The world's first official electrocutioner was Edwin F Davis, who went on to electrocute 240 other condemned criminals including the first woman to be electrocuted, Martha Place (*see 1899*).

❑ **ONLY** woman hanged for murder in Britain whose father had also been hanged for murder

Mary Eleanor Wheeler (Mrs Pearcey), Newgate Prison, London. Tuesday 23 December 1890

On 24 October 1890, 24-year-old Mary lured her lover's wife and one-year-old daughter to her home. There she murdered the wife by fracturing her skull with a poker and cutting her throat so violently as to nearly sever the head. She then pushed the body across several streets in the child's pram and dumped both bodies on wasteland. The daughter's body was unmarked, leading to speculation that Mary had put the mother on top of the child, suffocating her under the weight of her mother's body. Police established Mary's relationship with the victim's husband, Frank Hogg, and while they searched Mary's house she calmly played the piano – but she had blood stained clothing, scratched hands, and was wearing two wedding rings, one of which was identified as Phoebe Hogg's. Ten years earlier, on 26 November 1880, Mary's father Thomas Wheeler was hanged at St Albans prison for the shotgun killing of farmer Edward Anstree during a robbery. In the condemned cell Thomas wrote a letter to the farmer's widow apologising for what he had done and asking her forgiveness and prayers that his sins should not be visited on his wife or then fourteen-year-old daughter. Sadly this was not to be – Mary's execution took place on Tuesday 23 December. The guards and executioner reported that she accepted her punishment bravely but, due to the murder of the baby, Mary evoked little public sympathy and there was a cheer from the crowd of 300 as the flag was hoisted indicating that the execution was complete. Madame Tussaud's made a wax model of her for the Chamber of Horrors, and bought the pram from Frank Hogg.

☆ FIRST criminal caught by fingerprints

Francisca Rojas, Necochea, Argentina. Wednesday 29 June 1892

On the evening of 29 June 1892 Rojas, covered in blood, ran screaming to a neighbour's hut claiming that a rejected suitor, local ranch worker Pedro Ramón Velasquez, had murdered her six-year-old son and four-year-old daughter. She told police that she had seen Velasquez running from her hut, then entered and found both children battered to death. Police arrested the feeble-minded Velasquez who admitted that he had rowed with Rojas but denied murdering her children. The police chief had Velasquez tied up and laid beside the candlelit corpses of the children all night in the hope that this terrifying ordeal would elicit a confession. Then rumours began circulating that Rojas's lover had been heard to say he would marry her if it were not for the children, and the police chief turned his attention to forcing a confession from Rojas by spending the night around her hut banging the walls and howling like an avenging angel. Rojas was unmoved. Then the police chief contacted headquarters at La Plata, where a Croatian-born immigrant named Juan Vucetich was in charge. A keen student of the new science of fingerprinting, Vucetich had trained his officers to be on the look-out for such evidence. He sent Inspector Eduardo Alvarez to investigate and Alvarez soon established that Velazquez had a cast-iron alibi that had been ignored. While Alvarez was in Rojas's hut, the evening sun illuminated a bloodstained thumbprint on the bedroom door, which he promptly cut out. At the station he took Rojas's right thumbprint, and when it was shown to match the print from her door she confessed that she had battered her children to death with a stone which she had thrown down a well. Rojas was sentenced to life imprisonment and the Argentine police academy in La Plata was later named 'Escuela de policia Juan Vucetich'.

❏ **ONLY** woman judicially hanged in New Zealand
✳ **LAST** person executed in Invercargill Gaol

Minnie Dean, Invercargill Gaol, New Zealand. 08:00 Monday 12 August 1895

Minnie McCulloch was born in Scotland in 1847 and emigrated to New Zealand about 1871, marrying farmer Charles Dean about a year later. They settled down in large house but long afterwards it burned down and they were forced to live in a crude, self-built two-bedroomed house. To supplement the meagre family income Minnie became a baby farmer, offering a home to unwanted children, and the Deans lived in the tiny house with their adopted daughter Mary and an average of about ten children. On 29 October 1889, six-month-old May Irene died of convulsions, and the following March six-week-old Bertha Currie also died, apparently of natural causes. With suspicion rife, Minnie began advertising under aliases, and in April 1895 she took on a one-month-old girl named Eva from her grandmother Mrs Hornsby. Shortly afterwards, the child disappeared. Investigations were swift and successful. At first Minnie denied ever having seen the child but Mrs Hornsby identified her as the person who had collected the infant. Police then searched the house but found nothing until Constable Barrett noticed that in the garden a patch of soil was oddly dark and had cut flowers 'planted' in it – 18 inches beneath, he found a baby's foot. The bodies of three children were found, at least one of whom had died from poisoning by morphine, quantities of which were found in the house. Charles was cleared of any involvement and the overwhelming evidence against Minnie meant that she was convicted despite denying all charges. Asked on the scaffold if she had anything to say Minnie replied, 'No, except that I am innocent.' As the rope was adjusted around her neck her last words were 'Oh God, let me not suffer.' Nobody knows the real death count but six children in her care were known to have died, seven were supposedly 'adopted out' to people Dean refused to name, and newspapers estimated she may have killed twenty.

☆ FIRST motorist to be fined for speeding

Walter Arnold, Tonbridge, Kent. Tuesday 28 January 1896

On 20 January 1896 an off-duty policeman in Paddock Wood, Kent, was having his dinner when he spotted car car whizzing past his house at break-neck speed. The officer abandoned his food, hopped onto his bicycle and gave chase. Five breathless miles later he caught his quarry and booked him for exceeding the 2mph speed limit which had been introduced for towns and built-up areas in 1865. On 28 January Arnold, an agricultural engineer from East Peckham in Kent, was hauled before the beak at Tonbridge Police Court where the officer testified that Arnold had been travelling at about 8 miles per hour. The horrified magistrate fined the reckless Arnold one shilling (5p) plus costs. Although he now had a criminal record this did not deter Arnold's passion for motoring – he went on to become Britain's first manufacturer of petrol-driven cars.

✽ LAST triple hanging at Newgate Prison

Fowler, Milsom and Seaman, Newgate Prison. 9 June 1896

Henry Fowler and Albert Milsom were convicted of battering to death 79-year-old Henry Smith while attempting to get him to reveal the combination of his safe – which was actually empty. At their trial, as the death sentence was being announced, Fowler lunged at Milsom and attempted to strangle him. William

Seaman lived up to his name in becoming a seaman, but he also became a notorious criminal and was convicted of a double murder at Whitechapel. To prevent Fowler and Milsom from fighting on the scaffold, Seaman was placed between the two former accomplices, and as he took up his position on the drop Seaman remarked that it was the first time he had been a peacemaker. It was also the last.

✳ LAST triple execution in Britain

Phillip Matthews, Frederick Burden, Samuel Smith, Winchester Gaol. Tuesday 21 July 1896

The first time Phillip Matthews, Frederick Burden and Samuel Smith ever saw each other was on the gallows of Winchester Gaol. Matthews, a 32-year-old Teignmouth Council coachman, was twice married with a daughter Elsie from his first marriage. In 1895, while still married to his second wife, he met fifteen-year-old parlourmaid Charlotte Mahoney and bigamously married her, after which his second wife abandoned him and Elsie. In a callous attempt to remove the impediment to his new marriage, Matthews strangled six-year-old Elsie – but when her body was found in a local wood she proved a far greater impediment than she had been while still alive. Burden, a 24-year-old labourer from Southampton, was condemned for cutting the throat, on 7 April 1896, of his 38-year-old lover Mrs Angeline Faithfull, whom he claimed had not lived up to her name. And Smith, an eighteen-year-old soldier stationed at Farnborough Barracks with the 4th King's Royal Rifles, had shot Corporal Robert Payne in revenge for being put on a breach of discipline charge. At their joint execution Smith, the youngest, was the most self-possessed and the only one whose hanging created a hitch – the white hood became bloodstained when he bit his tongue in the fall.

☆ FIRST driver to be convicted of drink-driving

George Smith, Bond Street, London. 12:45 Friday 10 September 1897

At 12:45 on 10 September 1897, 25-year-old taxi driver George Smith, an employee of the Electric Cab Company, was spotted by PC Russell 247C erratically driving his taxi onto the pavement and into the front corridor of the home of Britain's most celebrated actor, Sir Henry Irving, at 165 Bond Street – one of London's most fashionable addresses. Smith was taken to Marlborough Street Police Court where he admitted having drunk 'two or three glasses of beer' and was fined twenty shillings.

☆ FIRST woman to be electrocuted
❏ ONLY woman electrocuted in the nineteenth century

Martha M. Place, Ossining, New York. 11:05 Monday 20 March 1899

By the time Martha earned her 'place' in criminal history 45 men had died in the electric chair. After working as housekeeper to widower William A Place, Martha Garretson married him and became stepmother to his devoted daughter Ida. An instant dislike between them ended on 7 February 1898 when Martha threw sulphuric acid in Ida's face then gloated as the seventeen-year-old thrashed about screaming in pain – Martha then attacked her with an axe before smothering her with a pillow. When William arrived home Martha fractured his skull with the axe but he managed to escape and call for help. When police arrived they found Martha attempting to gas herself. Her plea of insanity was rejected and she was sentenced to die in the electric chair, Governor Theodore Roosevelt personally refusing her plea for clemency and ordering the 'solemn and painful act of justice' to continue. Martha spent her last days reading the Bible, and when she she sat down in the chair she said, 'God help me.' The 1,760 volt surge loosed the Bible she still clutched in her hand. After four seconds the potential was reduced to 200 volts and kept steady for almost a minute, then one more short shock was applied and she was pronounced dead. The warden sent a telegram to Roosevelt: 'There was no revolting feature. Mrs Place met her fate with fortitude at 11:05 this morning.' Years later executioner Edwin Davis said Martha Place was, 'one of the coolest people I ever executed.'

☆ FIRST police car chase in Britain

Sgt Hector McLeod, Weedon Road, Northamptonshire. Thursday 27 April 1899

Barnum & Bailey's Circus 'The Greatest Show on Earth' – the biggest touring circus ever to be seen in Britain – was due to arrive in Northampton on 1 May 1899. Therefore it wasn't surprising when on 27 April a smartly-dressed man claiming to be from their advance publicity office came to town offering free tickets to shopkeepers in exchange for displaying advertising posters in their windows. The man explained that he would return the following day with the posters but meanwhile he needed a token sum of three shillings deposit for the tickets, which would be refunded at the box office. After a dozen successful acceptances he tried a shop owned by Jane Botterill, who grew increasingly suspicious and, after wisely refusing the offer, dashed to the St James End police station to report her concerns. Sergeant Hector McLeod took immediate action – after establishing that the man was walking west towards Weedon he decided the quickest way to catch the villain was to commandeer the 31/2 horsepower Benz-based motor car belonging to local tailor William Herbert Harrison, known as 'Jack', who was only the third person in Northampton to own a car. McLeod and Harrison sped off in pursuit of the unsuspecting swindler, who was apprehended on the road between Harpole and Flore and then chauffeured back to the police station in Angel Lane, Northampton. He was identified as Frederick John Phillips, an unemployed printer, and charged with obtaining ten shillings by false pretences and with twelve counts of selling counterfeit tickets; because he had no previous convictions he was later bound over to the sum of £10. It is not recorded whether McLeod and Harrison exceeded the then legal limit of 12 mph but ironically, the previous August, this very same car had been at the centre of the first ever prosecution for speeding in Northampton, when Joseph Grose was fined for driving it at 15 miles per hour in Wellingborough Road.

✳ LAST Wild West stagecoach robbery pulled by a woman

Pearl Hart, Near Benson, Arizona. Tuesday 30 May 1899

Hart, born Pearl Taylor in Ontario, Canada, was well-educated but naturally rebellious. At sixteen she eloped with William Hart in what proved to be a disastrous and violent marriage, and by the age of 21 was a cross-dressing, marijuana-addicted saloon singer and rumoured prostitute – although she insisted she was only 'good looking, and ready for anything that might come'. While working as a cook she met a prospector named Joe Boot, and between them they cooked up the plan to rob a stagecoach. On 30 May 1899 Boot and Hart, who was dressed in man's clothing and brandishing a rifle, forced Arizona's Benson-Globe stagecoach to stop. Witnesses described the bandit as more like a boy than a man: one said he was 'a terribly little fellow to be dragged into this criminal business', while another said he 'almost wished there was some way of letting him off with a good spanking.' Hart ordered the three passengers – a drummer, a dude and a Chinese gentleman – off the coach and robbed the drummer of $390, the dude of $36, and the Chinese man $5: a total of just $431. In fact she and Boot netted only $428 because Hart returned a dollar to each passenger to pay for food and lodgings when they reached Globe. She then took the driver's pistol and headed off with Boot but they got lost in a storm and three days later they were found (rather than caught) near Benson by the local sheriff. Boot was sentenced to thirty years in jail (he escaped in 1901 and was never heard of again), and Hart was sentenced to five, despite trying to convince the jury that she was temporarily insane because of a supposed desire to see her sick mother and children. She served two years of her sentence before being paroled in December 1902. After appearing in Wild West shows across the country as 'The Arizona Bandit', she married a rancher Calvin Bywater, with whom she lived a peaceful life until her death in December 1952.

☆ FIRST police car

Akron, Ohio. June 1899

The first police car was an electric wagon built by the Collins Buggy Co. in 1899 at a cost of $2,400. It weighed an incredible 5,500lbs including batteries, had three speeds with a top speed of 18 mph on level ground, and could run for thirty miles without recharging. Patrolman John Durkin had the honour of making the first motorised arrest when he picked up a drunk for being a public nuisance. The following year, on 22 August 1900, a mob hijacked the wagon during a fierce riot, drove it wildly through downtown Akron and finally dumped it into the Ohio Canal. Rescued the next day, it served a few more years before being junked. Patrolman Durkin, who went on to become Akron police Chief of Police, admitted that as an old-fashioned lawman he didn't trust automobiles, saying that he walked to work each day.

❑ **ONLY** man in the twentieth century to be hanged for murdering his own grandson

Joseph Holden, Strangeways Prison, Manchester. Tuesday 4 December 1900

After his wife's death, 57-year-old Holden moved in with Sarah Alice Dawes, one of his seven children. When Sarah evicted him for excessive drinking it was the final straw for Holden, who took his revenge on 5 September 1900 by murdering his nine-year-old grandson John Dawes and throwing the body into a quarry. 'I took him by the scruff of the neck and breeches, and threw him down the quarry. I then went down into the quarry to him. He seemed to be bleeding from the back of the head. I picked him up again and threw him into the water.' Death was from drowning.

❑ **ONLY** uncle and nephew to be executed in the United Kingdom

John Miller and John Robert Miller, Newcastle Prison. 08:00 Saturday 7 December 1901

Fairground ride operator John Miller was shocked to learn that his sister, a wealthy 85-year-old widow, had married a rascally itinerant showman named Joseph Fergusson. Fearing he would lose his inheritance, Miller persuaded his feeble-minded thirty-year-old nephew John Robert Miller to go with him to Fergusson's home in Cullercoats, Northumberland, where they stabbed him eight times in the neck, chest and hands. A double execution was planned, but then cancelled for fear that the nephew would attack his uncle on the scaffold – in the end, after spending his final night screaming with fear, John Robert Miller went to the scaffold ninety minutes before his uncle.

❏ ONLY private detective executed in Britain

William Lane, Stafford Gaol. Monday 11 August 1902

For eleven years William Lane had been a policeman in Bradford before setting up a private detective agency – a career change that would end in tragedy. In 1896, ex-dancer Elizabeth Dyson asked Lane to help her with her divorce and they soon became lovers. Recklessly, Lane invited her to become a lodger under the same roof as his wife and two sons. Unsurprisingly the arrangement didn't work. Lane asked Elizabeth to leave, then moved to West Bromwich with his family to start a new business. But Elizabeth followed and soon moved back in as lodger. Mrs Lane found the situation intolerable and on 20 June 1902 she left with her sons. Three days later, during a drunken row, Lane slashed Elizabeth's throat so violently that she was almost decapitated. The jury took just three minutes to convict. Lane's wife and sons visited him in the death cell, where they forgave him his sins.

☆ FIRST conviction of British criminal based on fingerprint evidence

Harry Jackson, Old Bailey, London. Saturday 13 September 1902

On 27 June 1902, while stealing billiard balls from a house in Denmark Hill, South London, Jackson left a thumbprint on a newly-painted window sill. Police took a photograph of the print and sent it to Scotland Yard for comparison with the fingerprint register that had been established on 1 July 1901. It was matched with 41-year-old Jackson, who had previously served time for burglary. Richard Muir (later Sir Richard) convinced a sceptical jury of the integrity of the new technology and on 13 September 1902 Jackson was sentenced to seven years' imprisonment.

❑ ONLY woman executed at Armley Jail

Emily Swann, Armley Jail, Leeds, West Yorkshire. 08:00 Tuesday 29 December 1903

Emily was unhappily married to glassblower William Swann. The unfortunate pair took in miner John Gallagher as a lodger and quickly she and John became lovers. The Swanns rowed frequently, and on 6 June William gave Emily two black eyes. This enraged Gallagher who fought with Swann and then told a neighbour, 'I'll murder the pig before morning. If he can't kick a man he shan't kick a woman.' A second fight ensued during which the neighbour heard Emily say, 'Give it to him, Johnny.' Ten minutes later neighbours saw Emily and John emerge showing 'every sign of affection' – inside the house behind them, William lay dead. John and Emily calmly went over to a friend's house and told them the situation. Emily was arrested but John went on the run for two months before being tracked down in Middlesbrough. In October 1903 the lovers were sentenced to death at Leeds Assizes. Emily seemed quite unperturbed and even smiled and kissed her hand to someone in the gallery. After sentencing the judge revealed that Gallagher had told police that William died after Emily had struck him with a poker. The only time the murderous lovers saw each other between sentencing and execution was at the prison chapel service on Christmas morning, where they were kept separate and not allowed to speak. On her final morning Swann was in a state of virtual collapse but after a drink of brandy she regained her composure and walked to the gallows where she said, 'Good morning, John.' The hooded and pinioned Gallagher, unaware of her arrival, was completely taken aback but managed to reply, 'Good morning, love.' As the noose was placed round her neck, Swann spoke her last words to her lover: 'Good-bye. God bless you.'

☆ FIRST British murder solved by fingerprint

Alfred and Albert Stratton, 34 High Street, Deptford, South London. 07:00 Monday 27 March 1905

Whilst burgling Chapman's Oil Shop in Deptford, the Strattons, aged 20 and 22, battered 69-year-old manager Thomas Farrow with a jemmy, knocking him unconscious. The noise woke Farrow's wife, 65-year-old Ann, whom they battered so ferociously that she died four days later without regaining consciousness. The Strattons then forced open a small cash box, which they mistakenly believed to contain the week's takings, and fled with the contents. Police found several clues including two stocking masks and the cash box, which carried a clear blood-stained thumb mark. Everyone who might have touched the box was eliminated, including the Farrows, who thus became the first corpses in England to have their prints taken. The print didn't match any of the 80-90,000 sets then at Scotland Yard but, realising that the need for masks probably meant the criminals were known to Farrow, police began to search for local villains. Seven days after the murder the Strattons were arrested and fingerprinted – Alfred's right thumbprint matched the print on the cash box. At their trial on 5 May 1905 the defence argued that fingerprint evidence was 'unreliable' being 'savoured more of the French courts than English justice'. The brothers were hanged side by side at Wandsworth Prison on 23 May 1905.

☆ FIRST police motorbike patrol

New York, USA. 1905

Established by New York City Police Department, with three bikes, the experiment was so successful that the department acquired twenty more the following year.

☆ FIRST celebrity trial of the twentieth century

Enrico Caruso, Yorkville Police Court, New York City. Tuesday 20 November 1906

Tenor Enrico Caruso was the world's first major recording star and one the most popular opera singers in history. On 16 November 1906 the 33-year-old superstar went to Central Park Zoo, where he was arrested in the Monkey House and accused of pinching a woman's bottom. He was taken to the Park Station protesting his innocence, then struggled with police before being bundled into a cell. The case became known as the The Monkey House Scandal and newspapers had a field day accusing Caruso of being 'an Italian pervert whose aim is to seduce innocent American ladies'. His two-day trial began on 20 November in the absence of the complainant Hannah K Graham, who had mysteriously vanished leaving a false address. The arresting officer, James J Kane, claimed Caruso had sidled up to three women and 'ogled them offensively', and that when he moved in on Hannah Graham and pinched her bottom she had struck him in the chest and screamed 'You loafer! You beast!' It was then that Kane made the arrest. None of the women mentioned was produced by the prosecution, and defence inquiries revealed that Kane had a track record of filing false charges at the Zoo – he also admitted to being a close friend of Hannah Graham, having been best man at her wedding. On the second day of the trial a mystery woman, dramatically veiled in white, testified that in February at the Metropolitan Opera House Caruso had brushed past her and fondled her breasts. Despite the lack of witnesses or corroborative evidence Caruso was denounced as a persistent molester of women, found guilty and fined $10. The conviction was upheld on appeal where Recorder Goff said it wasn't necessary for Mrs Graham to appear in court as 'the offence was not so much against the individual as against public order and decency.' Ironically Caruso's reputation was enhanced and his next appearance on the New York stage was a triumph. Knocko the monkey, outside whose cage the scandal erupted, became an overnight star and crowds flocked to see him but unfortunately it seems the attention was too much and he died, apparently from over-excitement.

☆ FIRST ASBO (though not named as such)

John Stone, Isle of Portland, Dorset. Wednesday 30 January 1907

Sixty-seven-year-old alcoholic John William Stone was banned for three years from all pubs and licensed clubs on the Isle of Portland, Dorset. This precursor of the modern Anti-Social Behaviour Order (ASBO) warned Stone that breaking the ban would incur a 20 shilling fine, rising to 40 shillings for further offences. Anyone caught selling him alcohol faced a £10 fine, increasing to £20 for further offences. Despite issuing his photograph and description – five feet four inches, of medium build with 'fresh' complexion, grey hair, grey eyes and grey moustache, broken nose and a limp – Stone (and subsequent drunkards) found it all too easy to obtain drinks and therefore the scheme was abandoned. In Edwardian times three convictions for being drunk and disorderly automatically labelled you 'a habitual drunkard'. (*See also 17 September 2004 for first modern ASBO*)

✳ LAST woman hanged in Wales

Rhoda Willis, Cardiff. Wednesday 14 August 1907

The last woman executed in Wales was not Welsh. She was born Rhoda Lascelles, the daughter of a respectable Sunderland hotel-keeper, but after losing her first husband her life quickly went downhill. A disastrous second relationship drove her to alcoholism; she then spent time in a workhouse, was imprisoned for theft, and finally sank into prostitution and baby farming. On 3 June 1907 a young mother, Maud Treasure, paid Willis £6 to adopt her child. Willis travelled home by train and managed to smuggle the baby into her lodging house but during the night she fell out of bed and awakened the landlady, Mrs Wilson, who went to her aid. She discovered Rhoda lying on the floor and noticed a bundle wrapped in a towel. Still in a drunken stupor, Rhoda mumbled, 'Hush, don't say anything! I'll get rid of it tonight.' Upon opening the bundle and discovering the dead body of a new-born baby, Mrs Wilson immediately informed the police. Willis claimed she had accidentally smothered the child while drunk, but she was convicted of murder and sentenced to death. The day before her execution she confessed to her solicitor that she had killed the child aboard the train. Earlier she had told a fellow prisoner, 'I thought once of drowning it in a bath, but afterwards decided to smother it. I squeezed it hard and some white stuff oozed from its mouth. I then wrapped it up and hid it.' She was executed on her 44th birthday by Henry Pierrepoint, who said she was the most beautiful women he ever hanged.

✳ LAST woman executed in Western Australia

Martha Rendall, Fremantle Jail, Perth, Australia. Wednesday 6 October 1909

In February 1907, 35-year-old Martha Rendall began working as housekeeper for carpenter Thomas Morris in East Perth, and soon became his common-law wife. To his five children she was the stepmother from hell, insisting they call her 'mother' and frequently thrashing them at the slightest provocation. Neighbours noticed the children had begun to look haggard and neglected. Two of them, Anne (nine) and Olive (seven) suffered sore throats and were prescribed throat swabs which Martha delighted in administering while the children screamed in agony. Anne soon died of 'diphtheria', followed three months later by Olive, also from 'diphtheria.' A year later Arthur (fourteen) died, with exactly the same symptoms, treatment and cause. Then, in 1909, George drank a cup of tea made by Martha that scalded his throat so badly she suggested a throat swab. Rather than face the agony suffered by his siblings George ran away from home, and when police were called in to find George, much overdue suspicions were voiced. An exhumation established that the throats of the three dead children had been washed with hydrochloric acid. Rendall and Morris were both charged with the three murders but Morris was acquitted. The night before her execution, history's most sadistic serial child killer received a visit from the children's father who, unbelievably, pledged his undying love to the vicious murderer of his three innocent children. After her execution, Rendall's body was buried in an unmarked pauper's grave. On 26 October 1964 the remains of Eric Edgar Cooke, the last man to be executed in Fremantle Prison, were buried in the same grave.

* LAST man to be executed in North Wales

William Murphy, Caernarfon, Wales. Tuesday 15 February 1910

On Christmas Day 1909, while having intercourse, Murphy strangled his unfaithful common-law wife then proceeded to cut her throat before pushing her body into a drainage ditch. On the day of Murphy's execution, hangman Henry Pierrepoint entered the death cell to find Murphy standing on a chair – Murphy jumped back down and said, 'I suppose it will be like that?' 'Yes,' replied the executioner, 'As easy as that.'

☆ **FIRST** criminal caught by wireless telegraph
❏ **ONLY** known murder by hyoscine

Dr Hawley Harvey Crippen, Father Point, St Lawrence Seaway, Canada. 09:00 Sunday 31 July 1910

Crippen's first marriage ended in 1882 when his wife, pregnant for the second time, suddenly and unexpectedly died of apoplexy. In 1892, having left his parents to bring up his son Otto, 30-year-old Crippen married nineteen-year-old would-be music hall singer Cora Turner (real name Kunigunde Mackamotski, stage name Belle Elmore). In 1897 the couple travelled to London to open an office for Crippen's employer selling patent medicines. The marriage was deeply unhappy, Cora making outrageous financial demands, frequently bringing men home for sex, and constantly belittling Crippen. Eventually Crippen began an affair with his secretary, Ethel Le Neve, 21 years his junior, and poisoned Cora with hydrobromide of hyoscine after a dinner party which finished at 01:30 on 1 February 1910. He then dismembered the body and buried it in the cellar of his house at 39 Hilldrop Crescent, Lower Holloway in London. He told Cora's friends that she had gone to America – later saying that she had died while travelling and been cremated – but they didn't believe him and reported their suspicions to Inspector Walter Dew at Scotland Yard. On Friday 8 July 1910 Dew interviewed Crippen and Le Neve (who was by then living in the family home as 'housekeeper') about Cora's disappearance. Crippen claimed she had left him to live with her lover in Chicago and that to avoid the shame he had told everyone she had died. Dew accepted the story, but remarked that Ethel was wearing one of Cora's brooches and that Cora had apparently left for her new life leaving behind a number of beautiful dresses – at which point Crippen decided to flee the country. On Monday 11 July, after a weekend reassessing Crippen's story, Dew was shocked to discover the house empty. A thorough police search uncovered human remains, and Dew immediately issued descriptions of Crippen and Le Neve. The pair had fled to Antwerp in Belgium, where on 20 July they boarded the steamship SS *Montrose*, bound for Canada. Crippen had shaved off his moustache, Ethel had cropped her hair and bought boys' clothing, and they were travelling together as Mr Robinson and his son, who was supposedly ill and travelling to Quebec for his health. Captain Kendall, the skipper of the *Montrose*, recognised Crippen from a newspaper photograph and telegraphed the ship's owners, who alerted Scotland Yard – the first time a ship-to-shore telegraph was used in a criminal case. Ironically, Crippen was heard admiring the wireless aerial and saying to his son John (actually Ethel) 'What a wonderful invention it is!' On 23 July Dew set sail on a faster ship, the SS *Laurentic*. The drama filled the newspapers of the time and was dubbed the 'crime of the century'. Finally the *Laurentic* caught up with the *Montrose* in Canadian waters. At 09:00 on 31 July 1911 Dew, dressed as a pilot, boarded the *Montrose* from the pilot's launch and arrested Crippen and Le Neve, who fainted. Crippen was tried at the Old Bailey and on 22 October the jury took just 27 minutes to convict. Inevitably, he was sentenced to death, and his petition for a reprieve was rejected by Winston Churchill. On 25 October Le Neve was tried before the same judge and acquitted. The night before his execution Crippen planned to commit suicide but was foiled when the death-watch warder discovered that he had removed an arm from his glasses with which to cut himself and painlessly bleed to death. His last request, which was granted, was to die with a photo of Le Neve in his top pocket. He was hanged in Pentonville Prison at 09:00 on Wednesday 23 November 1911, by John Ellis, who recalled: 'I could see him smiling as he approached, and the smile never left his face up to the moment when I threw the white cap over it and blotted out God's light from his eyes forever.' That same day Le Neve, under an alias, boarded a ship for America.

☆ FIRST murder in America solved by fingerprints

Thomas Jennings killed Clarence B Hiller, Chicago. Monday 19 September 1910

Hiller and his wife were awoken shortly after 02:00 by an odd sound, and Hiller found a stranger at the head of stairs. A fight ensued, both men fell down the staircase, two shots rang out and Hiller lay dead. Less than a mile away, four off-duty policemen waiting for a streetcar to take them home saw Jennings acting suspiciously. Finding a loaded revolver and fresh bloodstains on his clothes they took him to the station where they learned of the Hiller murder. Investigating officers found four fingerprints in fresh paint, which matched Jennings' fingerprints with 33 points of identity; and Jennings' revolver cartridges were identical to those found beside Hiller's body. Jennings' defence objected that fingerprint evidence was not recognised by the laws of Illinois, but he was nonetheless found guilty and sentenced to death. On 21 December 1911, after considerable legal wrangling, the Supreme Court of Illinois approved the legality of fingerprint evidence and the death sentence was upheld. The *Chicago Daily Tribune* stated: 'The circumstances of the negro's conviction were dramatic enough to furnish the "big scene" in a sensational novel.'

☆ FIRST get-away car used in a robbery

Bonnot Gang, Société Générale Banque, Rue Ordener, Paris, France. 08:25 Thursday 21 December 1911

The first ever getaway car was a 1910 Delaunay-Belleville luxury limousine with green and black trim and licence plate 783-X-3. It was stolen on 14 December 1911 by the four-man Bonnot Gang, who changed the plate to 668-X-8 and used the car a week later in a daylight attack on Monsieur Caby, a bank messenger en route to a branch of the Société Générale in the Rue Ordener, Paris. At 08:25 Caby arrived by tram carrying a satchel and a briefcase, and was met by a bank bodyguard. Gang members Octave Garnier and Raymond La-Science jumped out of the limo and headed straight for them. La-Science pulled out a gun and held it inches away from the face of the bodyguard who dodged past and ran into the bank. Garnier pushed the messenger to the ground and grabbed the satchel but Caby would not let go of the briefcase and was dragged along the street until Garnier fired three shots, two of which hit Caby in the chest. Jules Bonnot drove the getaway car level with the action and, after Garnier and La-Science had jumped in, executed a tyre-screeching U-turn and sped away, the gangsters firing warning shots. They raced north through France and abandoned the car on the beach near Dieppe Casino, leading police to believe they had fled to England. The satchel contained 5,500 francs and the briefcase some 130,000 francs-worth of unredeemable cheques and bonds. They had missed a wallet inside Caby's jacket containing 20,000 francs in cash. The following day Paris cinemas screened re-enactments of the historic robbery to musical accompaniments.

DID YOU KNOW?

Garnier was the gang leader but the press dubbed them the 'Bonnot Gang' after Bonnot, armed with a Browning automatic, appeared in the office of the daily newspaper *Petit Parisien* to complain about the paper's coverage of the gang. On 24 April 1912 Bonnot made a rooftop escape after shooting dead Louis Jouin, vice-chief of the Sûreté Nationale (French police). Four days later he was cornered in a Paris suburban house and surrounded by 500 armed police officers. The building was bombed and Bonnot was found riddled with ten bullets but still alive. Police Chief Louis Lepine killed him with a single shot to the head.

❑ ONLY New York City policeman executed for murder

Charles Becker, Sing Sing Prison, Ossining, New York. 05:53 Friday 30 July 1915

As a young patrolman in the 1890s Becker accepted bribes and extorted protection money from criminals, and in 1910 he became a lieutenant and expanded his protection racket to include brothels, nightclubs and gambling dens. Then, in 1912, casino boss Herman 'Beansie' Rosenthal refused to pay so Becker organised a raid during which the club was destroyed and money stolen. In revenge Rosenthal turned to Manhattan District Attorney Charles S Whitman, who had publicly promised to rid New York of corrupt cops, and exposed Becker as the key figure in an organised network of police graft known as The System. Becker then ordered his henchman Big Jack Zelig to have Rosenthal killed, and on 16 July 1912 four hired gunmen slew Rosenthal outside the Cafe Metropole on West 43rd Street. The getaway car was tracked down and Zelig confessed that Becker had orchestrated the killing. Zelig was shot before he could give evidence but Becker was nonetheless convicted. Five guards had to help the collapsing 43-year-old into the newly varnished chair, where 1,850 volts surged through him. A bright flame burst through his left temple and blazed for a full minute. A guard buckled the chest strap, which had been forgotten, then the current was turned loose for another ten seconds. There was still a heartbeat. The headpiece was removed and readjusted, and a third jolt was put through him. Finally, at 05:53, after nine minutes of agony, Becker was pronounced dead. Becker's wife, who had desperately pleaded for clemency from the new governor – none other than former DA Whitman – had a silver plate attached to Becker's coffin reading: 'Charles Becker, Murdered July 30 1915 by Governor Whitman.' In a final ironic touch, the hearse carrying Becker's fried corpse broke down when its engine overheated.

* LAST US stagecoach robbery
☆ FIRST US conviction based on palmprint evidence

Jarbidge, Elko County, Nevada. 18:30, Tuesday 5 December 1916 and Saturday 6 October 1917.

Jarbidge became a boomtown when gold was discovered in 1909 but remained isolated. Its nearest neighbour was 65 miles away and cars and trucks couldn't make the steep journey so even as late as 1916 gold had to be transported by mule and horse-drawn stagecoach. The last US stagecoach robbery took place during a fierce blizzard and the following morning, when the stagecoach hadn't arrived, a posse of anxious miners went in search of their payrolls. Only a quarter of a mile out of town they found the coach with the horses still hitched and nearly frozen to death. Federal mail-stage driver Fred M Searcey had been shot in the head and $3-4,000 in gold coins had been stolen. A violent struggle had taken place before Searcey had been shot, and bloody fingerprints and a palmprint were found on several pieces of mail. Drifter and ex-con Ben Kuhl was arrested with an accomplice, Bill McGraw, and at Kuhl's trial two fingerprint experts agreed that the palmprint belonged to Kuhl – the first time such evidence had secured a conviction in a US court. On 6 October 1907, after an eighteen-day trial, Judge EJL Taber sentenced Kuhl to death but a week before his scheduled execution he received a stay and was later sentenced to life imprisonment. The prosecutor, Edward P Carville, went on to become governor of Nevada and ironically it was he who released Kuhl on 16 April 1943 after he had served 25 years 6 months 10 days – longer than anyone else in the Nevada State Prison. Kuhl died soon afterwards and the money was never recovered. As it was obvious Kuhl hadn't had time to spend it people concluded that he had stashed it somewhere in the hills, and to this day treasure hunters travel to Jarbidge in search of Kuhl's hidden gold.

DID YOU KNOW?

Although Kuhl's crime was the last horse-drawn stage robbery in the nation, purists argue that it was not a 'stagecoach' but a buckboard-like wagon technically known as a 'mail stage'.

☆ **FIRST** case in British history of crime passionel, in which a guilty man is freed on grounds of self defence

Lt J Douglas Malcolm, Old Bailey. Tuesday 11 September 1917

On 14 August 1917 Lt Douglas Malcolm deliberately shot his wife's lover, Anton Baumberg – or 'the Count de Borch', as he liked to call himself. Malcolm fired four shots in four seconds, and the war was knocked into second place on the front pages by the sensational story of Lt Malcolm – 'a man of antique honour'; his wife Dorothy – 'a woman of great beauty'; and Anton Baumberg – 'an adventurer of Russian-Polish (and Jewish) extraction'. After the acquittal Douglas and Dorothy lived together unhappily ever after. Their only child was a son, Derek, who was born fifteen years later and became one of Britain's leading film critics. (An aunt later revealed that Derek's real father was the Italian Ambassador to London.)

❏ **ONLY** albino executed for murder in Britain

Joseph Rose, Oxford Prison. Wednesday 19 February 1919

Joseph Rose was a 25-year-old albino with the classic shock of white hair and pink eyes. He and his first cousin Sarah lived as husband and wife with their five-month-old daughter Isabella. On 28 October 1918 witnesses saw a blood-soaked Rose staggering along the inappropriately named Love Lane in Shawcum-Donnington, near Newbury in Berkshire. He claimed a casual acquaintance named 'Harry' had attacked him and his wife and daughter, whose bodies were found soon afterwards with their throats cut. Circumstantial evidence, and the failure to find 'Harry', condemned Rose to the gallows.

✳ LAST person imprisoned for blasphemy in Britain

John William Gott, Old Bailey, London. Friday 9 December 1921

Originally a tailor and draper, Gott became infamous as a freethought propagandist and publisher. Punishment did not deter him: he was imprisoned in 1911, sentenced to a total of eight weeks' hard labour in 1916 and 1917, fined and imprisoned in 1918, and sentenced to six months' hard labour in 1921. Shortly after his release he was summoned before West Ham police court on a charge of obstruction, later changed to blasphemy, for selling anti-Christian pamphlets. The case was heard at the Old Bailey on 9 December 1921 where, after a retrial, he was found guilty and received nine months' imprisonment with hard labour. In January 1922 the Lord Chief Justice dismissed an appeal, saying: 'It does not require a person of strong religious feelings to be outraged by a description of Jesus Christ entering Jerusalem "like a circus clown on the back of two donkeys".'

❑ ONLY British solicitor executed for murder

Herbert Rowse Armstrong, Gloucester Prison. 08:00 Wednesday 31 May 1922

Armstrong was a tiny five foot three inch, seven-stone, walrus-moustached solicitor who insisted that everyone call him Major after he was demobbed from the Royal Engineers in 1920. He was married to Katherine, a tall, teetotal hen-pecking hypochrondriac. In July 1920 Katherine became ill and for several months she suffered a wasting disease. She had made a will leaving everything to their three children, plus a tiny annual pension of £50 to her husband but, inexplicably, she suddenly reversed that will to leave everything to Herbert and neglecting the children. On 22 February 1921 Katherine died, officially from heart disease arising from nephritis and gastritis. A few months later, on 20 September, rival solicitor Oswald Martin received a 1lb box of Fuller's chocolates in the post from an anonymous well-wisher but, as neither he nor his wife enjoyed chocolates, they were put away until 8 October when Martin's two brothers and their wives visited – only Dorothy Martin ate chocolates and only she was violently ill during the night. Then, on 26 October, Martin went for tea at Armstrong's house to settle a land dispute in a friendly manner. Armstrong poured Martin a cup of tea and handed a scone to Martin with the apology, 'Excuse fingers.' Within a few hours Martin began vomiting and was ill for five days. The local doctor was at a loss for the cause until Martin's father-in-law, the town's chief chemist, recalled that Armstrong had recently purchased arsenic at his shop. The doctor immediately ordered an analysis of Martin's urine, which revealed that had ingested arsenic; the chocolates were then tested and also proved positive – and when Armstrong was arrested and charged with attempting to murder Martin police found a packet of arsenic in his pocket. Katherine's body was exhumed and when that too tested positive for arsenic Armstrong was charged with her murder. On 31 May 1922, on the scaffold of Gloucester Prison, he declared 'I am innocent of the crime for which I have been condemned to die.' On 9 November 1920, just 109 days prior to Katherine's death, another Welsh solicitor, Harold Greenwood, was acquitted of poisoning his wife – coincidence or inspiration?

* LAST Great American Train Robbery

Gold Special Train, Tunnel 13, Siskiyou Mountains, Oregon. 12:30 Thursday 11 October 1923

As Southern Pacific Railroad Train 13 from Seattle to San Francisco entered Tunnel 13 under the Siskiyou Mountains on the Oregon-California border, two grease-faced armed men jumped aboard the tender. At gunpoint they ordered engineer Sydney Bates (51) and fireman Marvin Seng (23) to stop the train when the locomotive, tender and mail car were clear of the tunnel, leaving the passenger coaches in the tunnel. A third gang member dynamited the side of the mail car but miscalculated the charge, destroying the mail car and incinerating mail clerk Edwin Daugherty – investigators found only his charred skull with a few vertebrae attached. The robbers panicked, shooting brakeman Coyl Johnson (37) as he ran to investigate, then shooting Seng twice and Bates in the back of his head before fleeing empty-handed. The gang left numerous clues, despite which police got nowhere. Eventually the investigating officers requested help from Dr Edward O Heinrich, a master criminologist known as 'The Edison of Crime Detection' because he ran an experimental crime laboratory at the University of Berkeley, California, and had a reputation for using Sherlock Holmes-type methods to solve crime. After studying the evidence Heinrich announced that their suspect was a left-handed lumberjack, approximately 25 years old, with brown hair, fair complexion, five feet eight inches tall, 165 pounds, and fastidious about his appearance. He explained that strands of hair and Douglas Fir needles had been recovered from overalls left at the scene, and that the garment was worn along its right side indicating a left-handed lumberjack who would lean his right side against trees while swinging his axe; the position of the braces clip indicated height and build, and nail clippings found in a pocket suggested fastidiousness. The robbers had filed off the serial number of a gun left at the scene but, unbeknownst to them (and to police investigators), the Colt Company put back-up numbers inside the handle – a secret Heinrich knew. The pistol was traced to 'William Elliott', a known alias of one Roy DeAutremont. In the overalls Heinrich also found a piece of paper overlooked by the police; a receipt for a registered letter, signed by Roy DeAutremont. There were three DeAutremont (aka D'Autremont) brothers: twins Ray and Roy, aged 23, and their younger brother Hugh, 19: all three were lumberjacks. Police distributed 2.5 million Wanted posters but it wasn't until 1927 that an American soldier recognised that fellow soldier 'James Price' was really Hugh. Soon afterwards the twins were located in Steubenville, Ohio, where, despite his bleached hair, Ray was recognised from newly-issued posters. On 24 June 1927 all three were sentenced to life imprisonment. After 26 years Roy went berserk and was given a prefrontal lobotomy in the same hospital used, years later, as the location for the feature film *One Flew Over the Cuckoo's Nest*.

❑ ONLY professional British footballer to be murdered

Tommy Ball, Brick Kiln Lane (now Beeches Road), Perry Barr, Birmingham. 22:15 Sunday 11 November 1923

Ball, 23, was Aston Villa's first-choice centre-half. He and his wife Beatrice rented one half of a semi-detached house from 45-year-old ex-policeman George Stagg, who lived in the other half. The relationship was strained because Ball kept a dog and chickens, both of which Stagg regarded as a nuisance, and in August 1923 Stagg gave them notice to quit. By November the Balls still hadn't left, and on Remembrance Sunday they went for a drink in their local pub, the Church Tavern. On their return Beatrice prepared a late supper while Tommy took the dog out for some exercise – but he got into an argument with Stagg and never returned. Stagg, who was carrying a single-barrelled bolt action 12-bore sporting gun, claimed that Ball was drunk and abusive and that he had initially fired the gun as a warning. He claimed that Ball had become even more aggressive and that a struggle had ensued during which the gun had accidentally exploded. Beatrice, on the other hand, claimed that the first shot had killed Tommy and that Stagg had fired the second shot at her while she was running for help. Stagg was sentenced to death but reprieved, and after three years' imprisonment he was declared insane and sent to Broadmoor. Tommy Ball's grave has a headstone shaped like a football.

☆ FIRST non-political killer hanged in the Republic of Ireland

William Downes, Dublin. Thursday 29 November 1923

Downes, 23, was a private in the newly created Irish Army. On 19 October 1923 he and an accomplice robbed the Ashtown Candle Factory in north Dublin, and when 22-year-old Detective Inspector Thomas Fitzgerald attempted to arrest them, Downes pulled a gun and shot Fitzgerald dead. Downes was hanged at Mountjoy Prison, where all of the Republic's 29 executions were carried out.

❏ ONLY time the rope broke during a British hanging in the twentieth century

Matthew Nunn, Durham Gaol. Wednesday 2 January 1924

Despite being pregnant, twenty-year-old Minetta Kelly refused to marry her lover, 24-year-old miner Matthew Nunn. At 02:00 on 12 September 1923 Nunn staggered into a friend's house with a badly gashed throat claiming that Minetta had attacked him with a razor then committed suicide by slashing her own throat. But Minetta's head was almost severed from her body, and it was obvious that her injuries were not self-inflicted. Police also found a suicide note written by Nunn, who believed he would die of his own self-inflicted wounds. Thomas Pierrepoint conducted the hanging, which resulted in a loud crash and a horrible thud with the snapped rope freely dangling. Nunn had landed heavily in the pit – still alive, though his jaw was 'horribly wrenched.' It took Pierrepoint 24 minutes to locate a new rope, reset the trap and hang the unfortunate Nunn for a second time.

☆ FIRST execution by gas chamber

Gee Jon, Carson City, Nevada. 09:40 Friday 8 February 1924

Gee Jon, a Chinese hatchetman, was found guilty of shooting a rival Tong man (ie Chinese gang member). The idea of execution by gas was proposed by toxicologist Dr Allen McLean Hamilton, who wanted to introduce the lethal gas silently into Gee Jon's cell while he slept. This proved impractical, so an improvised gas chamber was erected from the remnants of an old barber shop in the prison yard. The day before the execution the procedure was successfully tested on two cats by the newly created Gas Adviser to the State of Nevada, E B Walker, who was actually the secretary of the California Cyanide Company (which supplied liquefied gas for exterminating pests in orchards, warehouses and ships). Weeping openly, Gee Jon was bound to chair by two guards, one of whom was so anxious to leave that he rushed out of the chamber leaving his partner pounding on the door screaming to be released. At 09:40 hydrocyanic acid was pumped into the chamber by hand but unfortunately it was a cold morning, and the acid needed a temperature of 75 degrees Fahrenheit to turn to gas. A standby electric heater was turned on to raise the temperature, and Gee Jon was told that once he smelled 'rotten eggs' he should hold his breath, count to ten, and then take several deep inhalations. The cyanide took six minutes to kill him, and it was another three hours before it was considered safe to open the chamber.

❏ ONLY female official witness at a British hanging

John Keen, Duke Street, Glasgow. Thursday 24 September 1925

On 16 May 1925, 22-year-old Glasgow gangster John Keen fatally stabbed Indian clothes dealer Noorh Mohammed. Keen was part of a gang that had threatened Noorh with violence unless he handed over goods – and when Noorh refused a mob gathered outside the home of Sundi Din at 56 Water Street, Port Dundas, where Noorh had taken refuge. As they tried to break down the door Noorh rushed out using a broom to defend himself. Keen stabbed him twice in the chest while fellow gang member Robert Fletcher punched him. At the trial Fletcher was given seven years for culpable homicide (the Scottish equivalent of manslaughter) and Keen was sentenced to death. Keen burst into tears and complained that he had not received justice, to which Judge Lord Ormindale replied, 'See your lawyer about that.' Uniquely for a British hanging, a female magistrate was one of the official witnesses at Keen's execution.

☆ FIRST criminal use of a Thompson submachine gun

Frank McErlane, Western Avenue & 63rd Street, Chicago. Friday 25 September 1925

Chicago-born McErlane was widely considered to be the most dangerous gangster alive. His natural mental instability was aggravated by alcoholism, and when he heard that bootlegging rival Edward 'Spike' O'Donnell had invaded his territory, retaliation was inevitable. McErlane borrowed a Thompson submachine gun that a gangster had discovered on a trip to Colorado. As O'Donnell was strolling along Western Avenue, McErlane cruised past in a car and peppered the street with bullets. Amazingly O'Donnell escaped unharmed but although this first hit was unsuccessful, the underworld recognised the Thompson's potential – especially as it could be carried legally because it did not violate the city's concealable-weapon law. This incident may be considered the start of Chicago's reputation as the 'gangster capital of the world'.

☆ FIRST FBI agent killed on duty

Special Agent Edwin C Shanahan, Chicago. Sunday 11 October 1925

When police received a tip-off that 24-year-old professional car thief Martin J Durkin was planning to hide a stolen automobile in a certain Chicago garage several officers were sent to stake out the garage along with 27-year-old Special Agent Edwin C Shanahan. When Durkin arrived, Shanahan, who was temporarily on his own, attempted to arrest him but Durkin (who had previously wounded four officers to avoid capture) grabbed an automatic pistol from the front seat of the car and shot Shanahan in the chest – Shanahan returned fire but collapsed and died as Durkin escaped. A few weeks later police received information that Durkin and his moll would be visiting the moll's relatives. Again police attempted to ambush Durkin and again Durkin escaped, this time after killing one police officer and wounding another. Near dawn on 20 January 1926, FBI agents at St Louis, Missouri, were notified that Durkin and his moll were in a stateroom railway carriage of the Texas Special which was stopped at a small town near St Louis. FBI Agents and St. Louis City police detectives surrounded the train and dragged the desperate gunman from the stateroom before he had an opportunity to reach for the weapons which were in his luggage and overcoat. Because it did not become a federal offence to kill an FBI Special Agent until 1934, Durkin was tried in a state court and convicted of Shanahan's murder. He was sentenced to 35 years in the penitentiary at Joliet, Illinois, and given a further 15 years for his other violations. Durkin was 53 when he was 'released upon expiration of sentence'.

☆ FIRST mobster to conceal a gun in an instrument case

Samuzzo Amatuna, Chicago. Wednesday 11 November 1925

Samuzzo 'Samoots' Amatuna was a professional fiddle player who originated the use of a violin case to conceal a gun. A violent, vain man, he once shot dead the horse hitched to a Chinese laundry wagon in retaliation for the laundry scorching his shirts. On Friday 13 November 1925 he was ambushed and shot while sitting in a reclining barber's chair with a towel over his face. He was rushed to hospital where, on being told that he was dying, he asked to marry his fiancé – but death arrived before the maiden. After this shooting it became customary among barbers of gangsters to position their chairs facing the shop entrance.

☆ FIRST aeroplane bombing raid by criminals

Williamson County, Illinois. Friday 12 November 1926

During American Prohibition two rival Illinois alcohol-smuggling gangs, the Sheltons and the Birgers, were involved in a violent power feud notable for its military hardware, including machine guns and even home-made tanks. In November 1926 a plane flew low over Charles Birger's farmhouse (real name Shachna Itzik Birger) and the pilot dropped three crude bombs precisely on target – fortunately for the occupants the bombs failed to explode.

☆ FIRST escape from Strangeways Prison

John 'Ruby' Sparks. Strangeways Prison, Manchester. 1927

Notorious burglar Sparks was a serial escaper, having previously escaped from borstal and later becoming the first to escape from Dartmoor (*see 10 January 1940*). He earned his nickname after burgling the Park Lane apartment of an Indian maharajah and swagging £40,000 worth of uncut rubies – which he gave away thinking them fakes! Sentenced to three years for another burglary he was sent to Strangeways, where a warder told him: 'Nobody has ever escaped from here.' A fortnight later he began his escape, paying £400 in bribes and buying up mailbag thread, blankets and a knife. Having made a dummy out of a stool, a blanket and a chamber pot, he donned a suit made from another blanket (his clothes had been taken from him) and then used the knife to saw through the cell bars and escape. He left a poem in the bed:

> The Cage is Empty
> The Bird is Flown
> I've gone to a Place
> Where I'm better Known'.

He said later, 'I signed it so the screws would know it was me who had escaped and not Shakespeare.'

☆ FIRST armoured truck hold-up in US

Flatheads Gang, Bethel Road, near Coverdale, Pennsylvania.
Friday 11 March 1927

An armoured truck carrying the $104,250 payroll of the Pittsburgh Terminal Coal Company blew up when it passed over a mine planted by the Flathead Gang. Five guards were injured and the gang escaped.

☆ FIRST photo of a woman dying in electric chair

Ruth Snyder, Sing Sing Prison, New York. 23:00 Thursday 12 January 1928

On 19 March 1927 Snyder managed to kill her husband at the eighth attempt after trying gas, narcotics and poisoning in the hopes of collecting $95,000 insurance money. Finally, assisted by her lover Henry Judd Gray, she attempted to crush her husband's skull with a sash weight. Despite being battered and chloroformed it wasn't until he was strangled with picture wire that he eventually died. Snyder received 164 offers of marriage from men wishing to be dominated by her. She and Gray were executed on the same day in the same chair, whose makeshift headpiece was a cut-down American football helmet lined with sponge. Snyder almost collapsed at the sight of it, and as she was strapped in she cried out, 'Father, forgive them for they not what they do.' She took seven minutes to die. One of the press witnesses, a *New York Daily News* staffer named Basil Gray (no relation to Snyder's lover) secretly attached a miniature camera to his leg with a trip line running to his wrist, and at the moment the current was thrown he snapped her lunging forward. The photo formed the full front page of the next day's *Daily News*, under the banner headline DEAD! At 23:10 Gray entered the death chamber and four minutes later he too was pronounced dead.

☆ FIRST ransom kidnapper in the US to be executed

William Hickman, San Quentin Prison. 10:10 Friday 19 October 1928

Needing $1500 to pay for tuition fees at a school of divinity, Hickman decided kidnapping could raise the funds to help him become a Minister. On 15 December 1927 he abducted Marian

Parker, one of the twelve-year-old twin daughters of Perry M Parker, the chief clerk of a Californian bank. He began sending ransom notes via telegram, signing himself 'The Fox', and Parker agreed to pay up. Then, following instructions he later said were spoken to him by God, Hickman strangled the little girl with a dish towel, severed her arms and legs, rouged her cheeks and wired her eyelids open using minute strands of picture-wire. He covered her torso with her school dress, draped her sweater over the dress and then propped the torso up in the back of his car before driving to the agreed drop-off point. Parker saw his daughter in the half light and paid over the ransom, at which Hickman threw the mutilated corpse onto the pavement. Over the next few days six parcels were found scattered around Los Angeles containing different parts of Marian's body. Hickman's gruesome hanging caused three of the 250 witnesses to faint – as the trap opened Hickman passed out, causing him to fall horizontally and bang his head on the side of the scaffold. Then, at the end of the drop, his body was jerked upright and began circling in a hideous fifteen minute death spiral as he slowly strangled, his hands twitching throughout.

❏ ONLY double execution in Washington's history

Walter Dubuc and Harold Carpenter, Thurston, Washington. Friday 15 April 1932

Carpenter, Dubuc (who claimed to be only sixteen years old) and their accomplice, mother-of-two Ethel Willis, planned to rob 85-year-old farmer Peter Jacobsen at his homestead in Walla Walla. During the raid Dubuc struck Jacobsen and Carpenter then bludgeoned him to death with the butt of a rifle. Both men were sentenced to death and Willis to life imprisonment. Carpenter sneered at the fifty witnesses to their double execution but Dubuc was half-carried to the scaffold crying, 'Don't let them hang me.'

✳ LAST man executed for rape in Australia

David Bennett, Australia. Monday 26 September 1932

In 1911 Bennett was sentenced to life imprisonment for rape but released after serving only six years. He then teamed up with Angus Murray to become an armed robber, a short career which ended in a fifteen-year sentence. However, both of them escaped six years later, in 1923. Bennett was quickly recaptured, serving out the rest of his sentence, but Murray went on the run and murdered a man during a botched bank robbery, for which he was caught and hanged in 1924. Within days of completing his sentence and being released in 1932 Bennett committed the outrage for which he was executed – the rape of a four-year-old girl.

❑ ONLY person prosecuted under the Honours (Prevention of Abuses) Act.

Maundy Gregory, Bow Street, London. Thursday 16 February 1933

In 1917 the British Liberal government appointed Gregory (a failed teacher, actor and theatrical agent) as its freelance 'Honours Broker'. The job entailed Gregory ingratiating himself with the rich and powerful and persuading them to part with money in exchange for honours – with substantial commissions for Gregory, who passed himself off as a rich publisher. Between 1916 and 1922 more than 1,500 knighthoods were awarded, 120 hereditary peerages created and the OBE initiated, of which 25,000 were awarded in four years. Rates included £10,000 for a knighthood (the equivalent of £0.25 million in 2005), £25,000 for a baronetcy and more than £50,000 for a peerage. When Gregory began broking honours the trade wasn't illegal but a 1925 Act of Parliament made it so, despite which Gregory surreptitiously continued flogging ermine to the determined. His downfall was trying to sell a title to incorruptible war hero Lieutenant Commander Billyard Lake, who denounced him. Gregory was fined £50 and given a six-month prison sentence, of which he served two. On his release he moved to France, where he died in a prison camp during the Nazi occupation.

❏ ONLY criminal officially declared Public Enemy Number One by the FBI

John Dillinger. Friday 22 June 1934

On John Dillinger's 31st birthday, 22 June 1934, J Edgar Hoover declared him the FBI's first 'Public Enemy Number One'. The following day the federal government promised a $10,000 reward for his capture, and a $5,000 reward for information leading to his arrest. Oddly enough, at that time the only federal offence Dillinger had committed was crossing a state line in a stolen car – but the notoriety gained through the national publicity of being declared Public Enemy Number One turned a small-time crook into a legendary gangster. Dillinger was killed thirty days later. Hoover did not invent the phrase 'public enemy': Chicago Crime Commissioner Frank L Loesch used it in the the early part of 1930, and by the end of that year bootlegger Irving 'Waxey' Gordon was being called Public Enemy Number One by New York newspapers. Dillinger remains the only person to have been officially named as such by the FBI.

DID YOU KNOW?

Gordon was nicknamed 'Waxey' because he started out as a pickpocket who could slide a victim's wallet out of his pocket as though it were coated in wax.

* LAST man in Scotland to be shackled in a prison cell
☆ FIRST inmate to escape from Peterhead Prison

Johnny Ramensky, Aberdeenshire, Scotland. December 1934

The 29-year-old safebreaker made the first ever escape from Peterhead Prison after being refused permission to attend his wife's funeral. In the early hours of a freezing morning he picked the door of the hospital block, where he was being held for depression, then, barefoot, he scaled the twenty foot gate and headed south to Glasgow, 170 miles away. He was captured just fifteen miles from his goal and taken back to Peterhead, where he was shackled to the walls for several weeks until John McGovern MP heard about his case and insisted the shackles were removed. Ramensky escaped from Peterhead four more times, causing Nicholas Fairburn QC to note that Ramensky had a lifelong compulsion to break into whatever he was out of and out of whatever he was inside. Ramensky became a folk hero, with two songs written about him: actor Roddy McMillan's 'Set Ramensky Free' and MP Norman Buchan's 'The Ballad of Johnny Ramensky'. He died on 4 November 1972 after spending more than 40 of his 67 years behind bars. During his final court appearance, after being caught during a roof-top break-in, Ramensky's solicitor said that he had been on more roofs than the legendary fiddler.

❑ ONLY murder case instigated by a shark

Coogee Beach Aquarium, Sydney, Australia. Thursday 25 April 1935

The name of Coogee, a Sydney beachside suburb, is derived from the Aboriginal koojah, meaning 'smelly place' or 'stinking seaweed', referring to the kelp washed up on the beach. On 17 April 1935 a local fisherman hooked a small shark, and when a four-metre tiger shark grabbed the smaller shark the fisherman caught that too. He took the tiger shark to the Coogee Beach Aquarium, where he thought it would make a wonderful attraction for the Anzac Day celebrations on 25 April. But onlookers were shocked when the shark disgorged a human arm, emblazoned with a tattoo of two boxers. Police took fingerprints and identified them as belonging to James Smith of Gladesville, a forty-year-old former boxer, bankrupt builder and small-time crook whose wife had reported him missing while they were on holiday in a rented seaside cottage. But the arm had not been bitten off by the shark – it had been severed by a knife some time after death, so police opened a murder investigation. Smith had last been seen on 9 April drinking with his best friend, forger Patrick Brady, in a pub at Cronulla. Brady denied any involvement in the death but mentioned the name of Reg Holmes who, when police interviewed him, denied even knowing Brady. Three days later police found Holmes with a bullet wound to the head – now he broke down and claimed Brady had killed Smith then disposed of the body. Brady was arrested but on the eve of the coroner's inquiry Holmes was found shot dead in a car near the Sydney Harbour Bridge. Without a complete body, and with Holmes' testimony not allowed as evidence, the judge directed the jury to acquit Brady, who died in August 1954 taking the truth behind Smith's death to the grave – only the shark was talking.

✷ LAST person publicly executed in Kentucky

Rainey Bethea, Owensboro, Kentucky. 05:30 Friday 14 August 1936

On 10 June 1936 Bethea, a 22-year-old Negro, broke into a house where he raped and murdered a 71-year-old white woman; he was caught after leaving his ring at the crime scene. According to Kentucky state law it was the county sheriff's job to hang a condemned criminal but the Owensboro county sheriff was a woman, Florence Thompson, who had become sheriff by default due to the death of her husband three days before Bethea's conviction. Local man Arthur Hash offered his services but unfortunately, despite it being a dawn execution, Hash turned up drunk and stumbled around the scaffold before locating the lever that sent Bethea to his doom. An estimated 15,000 people were disappointed, having turned up to see Florence become America's first female executioner, and angry newspapers misreported that she fainted on the scaffold. It took fifteen minutes for Bethea to slowly strangle to death, during which time ghoulish members of the crowd crushed forward, snatching pieces of his clothing and even cutting pieces of flesh as souvenirs. Most reference works give this as the last public execution in the United States but recent research shows this to be untrue. (*See 21 May 1937.*)

❏ ONLY dwarf executed in Britain in the twentieth century

Max Mayer Haslam, Strangeways Prison, Manchester. Thursday 4 February 1937

In burgling the Lancashire home of Ruth Clarkson, Haslam battered the 74-year-old widow seventeen times with a tyre lever. During the attack her dog bit Haslam so he hanged it from her bedpost before leaving with jewellery and £200 cash.

✳ LAST official public hanging in the United States

Roscoe Jackson, Stone County, Missouri. 06:03 Friday 21 May 1937

On 2 August 1932, travelling salesman Pearl Bozarth picked up hitchhiker Roscoe 'Red' Jackson in Taney County – Jackson repaid the kindness by killing Bozarth and taking his car and money. He was soon arrested and condemned, and his execution was set for early in the morning to minimise the crowds. Jackson's last words from the scaffold were to the assembled crowd: 'Everyone has to die and I am going to die like a man.' IH Coin, the sheriff in charge, failed in his effort to prevent a Fox Movietone cameraman from filming the event. It was the only execution at which Coin officiated and according to his family he never recovered from the ordeal; he committed suicide a few months later.

DID YOU KNOW?

In 1934, two years after Jackson's hanging, Pennsylvania became the first US state to outlaw public hangings.

☆ FIRST woman to die in the electric chair in Ohio

Anna Hahn, Ohio. 7 December 1938

Thirty-year-old Hahn made a living nursing elderly gentlemen, and people began to notice that her income was heavily supplemented by the bequests many of them left in their wills after they died despite her tender care. Police were alerted and exhumations ordered. Poison was found, and when police chief Patrick Hayes searched her house he found 'enough poison to kill half of Cincinnati' – she is estimated to have killed between five and fifteen men using arsenic and strychnine. Convinced that she would be reprieved, Hahn remained calm until the day of her execution, when four guards were needed to forcibly carry her to the chair and strap her in as she screamed, 'Don't do this to me. Think of my boy. Can't you think of my baby? Isn't there anybody who will help me?'

* LAST person publicly guillotined in France
❏ ONLY public execution carried out by executioner
Henri Desfourneaux

Eugene Weidmann, Rue Georges Clemenceau (in front of the the
Palais de Justice), Versailles. 04:50 Saturday 17 June 1939

Asked if he felt any remorse at the six murders of which he had
been found guilty, Weidmann replied 'Remorse, what for? I didn't
even know them.' On the eve of his execution every vantage point
overlooking the guillotine was rented out at fantastic prices and
from his cell, while his hair was trimmed and his shirt collar cut
away, Weidmann could hear the laughter of revellers awaiting the
entertainment. Executioner Henri Desfourneaux began setting up
the guillotine at 03:00 for a dawn execution but due to delays and
miscalculations it was broad daylight by the time the blade fell.
Weidmann, fortified by a few puffs on a cigar and a mouthful of
rum, was led to the guillotine and strapped to the bascule (the see-
saw plank which tips horizontally to load the victim under the
blade). But Desfourneaux had set the bascule badly, and after three
attempts to get Weidmann's neck into the lunette (the crescent-
shaped head-holder) the assistant executioner had to pull him
forward by his hair and ears. When the blade finally dropped at
04:50, Weidmann's body emitted the eerie whistling sound often
heard at beheadings – the neck emits a gasp as the last breath leaves
the lungs, even though the head is already in the basket.
Desfourneaux's botched measurements meant that as well as
decapitating Weidmann the blade also chipped his chin. One
horrified witness spoke of 'a geyser of blood' and another of
Weidmann's 'staring eyes'. The fact that the execution took place in
daylight enabled photographers to take shockingly clear pictures,
which so affected the public that a statute was passed a week later
decreeing that all future executions would be carried out in private.

☆ FIRST successful escape from Dartmoor Prison
☆ FIRST British 'Public Enemy Number One'

John 'Ruby' Sparks, Dartmoor Prison. 10 January 1940

Unable to steal the five keys he needed to escape, Sparks memorised the pattern of each one in a feat of mental photography. It took the 38-year-old Camberwell burglar a year to make the keys, using metal secretly removed from the machine shop, after which he simply let himself out. His audacious escape earned him the distinction of being the first British criminal to be named 'Public Enemy Number One', having also been the first man to escape from Strangeways Prison (*see 1927*). Sparks never escaped again, but his Dartmoor record of 170 days on the run has never been bettered.

☆ FIRST execution by America's only portable electric chair

Willie Mae Bragg, Lucedale, Mississippi. Friday 11 October 1940

Wife-killer Bragg was the first victim of a bizarre method of execution carried out by an even more bizarre executioner, Jimmy Thompson. Thompson, 44, was a heavily tattooed ex-sailor whose stage career as Dr Zogg the turbanned hypnotist (aka Dr Stingaree and Dr Alzedi) ended when he was imprisoned for highway robbery. Pardoned in 1939 and appointed executioner in 1940 by his friend and bird-shooting companion Governor Paul B Johnson, Thompson began touring the length and breadth of Mississippi executing convicted criminals for $100 a hit. The reason Thompson was an itinerant executioner was that in order to avoid any one county becoming known as Mississippi's 'execution capital', the state commissioned a portable electric chair. Built in September 1940 at a cost of $4,000, it consisted of a huge silver truck carrying a portable generator and a strong wooden chair complete with straps, electrodes and helmet. Five of Thompson's first nine clients were offered the alternative of hanging, and Thompson (who boasted his 'fry parties' were never spoilt by sparks or scorched flesh) was so pleased at their choice that he told them: 'I'm going to show my appreciation by giving you a nice clean job. I'm going to give you the prettiest death a guy can have.'

✳ LAST execution in the Tower of London

Josef Jakobs, Tower of London, Tower Hill, London. 07:12 Friday 15 August 1941

Jakobs was a German spy born in Luxembourg. On 31 January 1941 members of the British Home Guard spotted him parachuting into a wooded area of Stifford, Essex, and had no trouble arresting him as he broke his ankle on landing. Found among his possessions were a wireless transmitter, forged identity papers and, most incriminating of all, a cold German sausage. After refusing to act as a double agent, Jakobs was court-martialled and sentenced to death despite not actually having committed espionage. The fifteen other spies executed in Britain during World War II were hanged in civil prisons, but for unspecified reasons Jakobs was sentenced to die by firing squad in the Tower of London. He was locked in a tiny cell within the Waterloo Barracks, which now houses the Crown Jewels, and at 07:00 on 15 August he hobbled to a miniature rifle range on the east side of the inner wall. Because of his broken ankle he was tied to an old Windsor chair rather than being made to stand, and a piece of white lint was pinned over his heart as a target for the eight man firing squad of Scots Guards. At 07:12 five of the eight shots hit their target. The condemned cell is now used to store film and, though not on public view, the death chair remains in the Tower.

☆ FIRST execution at which Albert Pierrepoint was Number One executioner

Antonio 'Babe' Mancini, Pentonville. Friday 31 October 1941

The first two men that Pierrepoint was scheduled to execute as Number One both had their appeals go all the way to the House of Lords. In 1935 Reginald Woolmington was successful. But Mancini, the 39-year-old manager of The Palm Beach Bottle Party Club in Soho, was not so lucky – his appeal was rejected and he was sentenced to hang for the fatal stabbing of Harry Distleman during a brawl. Pierrepoint, at 26 the youngest person present, went through the routine that was to serve him for another 23 years: 'Cap, noose, pin, lever, drop...' As Pierrepoint placed the white hood over the condemned man's head, Mancini spoke his last word – 'Cheerio'.

☆ FIRST woman executed in the gas chamber
☆ FIRST legal execution of a woman in California

Juanita Spinelli (aka Ethel, Eithel Leta, Elizabeth and Evelita Spinelli), San Quentin, California. Friday 21 November 1941

Prosecutors described 52-year-old Spinelli, the head of an underworld gang, as a 'scheming cold, cruel woman'. Known as The Duchess, this ex-wrestler and knife thrower, who could pin a poker chip at fifteen paces, was executed for helping two members of her gang drug and murder a fellow gang member who they thought was about to inform on them. Spinelli arrived at the octagonal, apple green gas chamber wearing a short-sleeved dress with a picture of her children and grandson strapped beneath it. She announced that it was not Christian to kill and prophesied about her executioners, 'My blood will burn holes into their bodies. Before six months have passed they will be punished.'

Executioners then dropped a 1lb bag of cyanide pellets into nine pints of 1:2 sulphuric acid and water, with 'a muffled "clunk" such as old plumbing sometimes makes'. Spinelli breathed in the noxious gas and coughed 'like an asthmatic', exhaling 'with a sound like that a horse sometimes makes with his lips'. Ten minutes and 14.5 seconds later she was dead, the 21st person and the first woman to die in California's gas chamber. The *Los Angeles Times* ran an editorial about her execution, which attracted 67 witnesses, under the headline 'Good Riddance'.

(*The first woman to be executed in California was another Juanita, but it is doubtful whether her hanging by a vigilante mob can be described as California's first legal execution. See 5 July 1851.*)

❑ ONLY case in which two rattlesnakes were used as murder weapons
✳ LAST man hanged in California

Robert James, San Quentin, California. Friday 1 May 1942

In a murderous insurance scam, barber and long-term con artist Robert James (real name Major Lisenba) convinced his pregnant wife Mary that she should undergo an illegal abortion. His accomplice Charles Hope posed as a doctor, insisting that Mary be drunk to ease the pain, gagged to prevent her arousing neighbour's curiosity, and blindfolded so she could not recognise him in the event of a trial. He then strapped her to the kitchen table and thrust her leg into a box containing two deadly rattlesnakes named Lethal and Lightning, expecting them to bite and kill her. But the whiskey acted as an antidote, so after several hours watching her writhing in agony Robert drowned Mary in the bath. Then he placed her head first in the fish pond, making it look as if she had tripped and drowned. The coroner returned a verdict of accidental death but the insurance company tipped off police that James' previous wife had also died 'accidentally'. Hope was given a life sentence and James condemned to death. His hanging was botched (it took him ten minutes to die), and Clinton Duffy, the warden of San Quentin, said afterwards: 'I wish everyone in California had seen it. I wish they seen the flesh torn from Lisemba's face by the rope and his half severed neck and his popping eyes and his swollen tongue. I wish they had seen his legs swinging and smelt the odours of his urine and defecation and sweat and caking blood.' After this botched hanging the state converted to gas.

☆ **FIRST** British murder conviction based on palmprint evidence

Samuel Dashwood and George Silverosa, Hackney Road, Shoreditch, London. 21 July 1942

On 30 April 1942, two men attacked 71-year-old pawnbroker Leonard Moules in his shop in Hackney Road, Shoreditch, battering him repeatedly with the butt of a gun – he died three days later. The thieves ransacked the safe, leaving behind a palmprint which didn't match any of the 4,000 then held by Scotland Yard. Following a tip-off, police arrested two local criminals, 22-year-old Dashwood and his sidekick Silverosa. The palmprint belonged to Silverosa and the gun belonged to Dashwood, so both were forced to admit being at the robbery but each blamed the other for the killing. Both were condemned to death on 21 July, at the end of a dramatic Old Bailey trial in which Dashwood sensationally dismissed his counsel, claiming that to do so was evidence of insanity and therefore any guilty verdict must be quashed. The judge, Mr Justice Wrottesley, disagreed, rightly refusing to set a precedent whereby any defendant with a hopeless case could dismiss their barrister and claim insanity. A few days before their double hanging Silverosa asked to incinerate some private papers. On arriving at the furnace he snatched a poker, attacked and severely injured both guards, and made an unsuccessful bid to escape. Dashwood and Silverosa were hanged side by side on 10 September 1942.

✷ LAST person sentenced under the British Witchcraft Act

Helen Duncan, Court No 4, Old Bailey, London. 10:30 Monday 3 April 1944

As a child, Scottish-born Helen earned the nickname Hellish Nell for her tomboyish exploits. She alienated her peers with bizarre behaviour and sinister predictions, and her mother predicted that one day she would be burnt as a witch. In 1916 Helen married invalided soldier Henry Duncan, whom she had 'first met in her dreams', and Henry neglected his business of cabinet-making to help her develop as a psychic and to help raise their six children. Helen's spirit guide was 'Albert Stewart', a sardonic Scots émigré to Australia; he was frequently accompanied by 'Peggy' who danced, sang and swung from curtain rails. Mrs Duncan became hugely popular as a medium, and even more so when she mastered the production of 'ectoplasm' from her nose and mouth – and even when this was exposed as a simple piece of vaudeville chicanery her popularity seemed to increase. Despite being fined £10 for fraudulently procuring money from members of the public demand for her services increased, and by 1944 she was a twenty-stone, chain-smoking, hard-drinking superstar who swore like a fishwife. On 25 November 1941, Helen's 44th birthday, a German submarine sank HMS *Barham* in the Mediterranean, killing 868 men. Not long after, at one of Helen's seances in Portsmouth, a dead sailor materialised for his mother clearly wearing a cap banded with the name HMS *Barham*. This was a great shock to the woman, because for morale purposes the Admiralty had withheld all information about the fate of the *Barham*. The following morning the desperate mother telephoned the Admiralty for confirmation and two officers interviewed her, wanting to know the source of her information. The authorities, which were already prosecuting mediums for exploiting the bereaved, were concerned a medium, and Helen in particular, might betray details of the D-Day preparations. On 19 January 1944 Helen was arrested during a seance, and on 23 March she was tried for 'pretending to raise the spirits of the dead' – an offence under the 1735 Witchcraft Act, which was not repealed until 1951. Many of the 45 defence witnesses amazed the packed courtroom with accounts of tearful reunions with deceased relatives, and Helen's offer to hold a seance in court – declined by the jury – caused a sensation. When the recorder gaoled Mrs Duncan for nine months the fur-coated witch screamed: 'I didn't do anything!' and promptly collapsed. An appeal failed and she served six months in Holloway Prison.

DID YOU KNOW?

After her release, Duncan (*above*) returned to mediumship, and in 1956 police stormed a materialisation seance in Nottingham. They ripped 'ectoplasm' from her, after which she displayed strange burns where the ethereal material had supposedly rushed back into her body. Police did not press charges and Helen returned home to Edinburgh, where she died six weeks later on 6 December 1956 – officially of diabetes and cardiac failure, though her family insisted she died of the trauma of ectoplasm not being allowed to finish its journey. In 1997 British spiritualist mediums launched a campaign to obtain a pardon for Helen, and in January 1998, at a spiritualist church in Castleford, she apparently materialised with a raised glass, toasting their efforts.

✻ LAST execution by firing squad in Great Britain

Benjamin Pyegate, Shepton Mallet Prison, Somerset. Tuesday 28 November 1944

A drunken brawl broke out among four US servicemen at the Drill Hall Camp, West End Road, Westbury. The four American soldiers grew increasingly violent until finally Benjamin Pyegate and James E Alexander squared up to one another. Pyegate kicked Alexander in the groin and as he doubled up and bent forward Pyegate whipped out a knife and stabbed him in the neck, killing him instantly. Pyegate became the second and last American to be executed by firing squad at Shepton Mallet Prison.

☆ FIRST criminal caught after police broadcast the phrase 'help with their inquiries'

Donald Thomas, 16 Mayflower Road, Clapham, South London. Tuesday 17 February 1948

On 13 February 1948, shortly after 20:00, plain clothes constable Nathaniel Edgar questioned 23-year-old Donald Thomas, who had been acting suspiciously in the driveway of 112 Wades Hill, North London. As Edgar took down details Thomas shot him three times and Edgar died an hour later in North Middlesex Hospital. His last notebook entry referred to 'Thomas, Donald, 247 Cambridge Road, Enfield.' Scotland Yard's public information officer, former BBC press officer Percy Fearney, wrote a historic radio appeal: 'Police urgently wish to interview Donald George Thomas, who is believed to be able to help them with their inquiries.' The announcement was heard by Stanley Winkless, who informed police that Thomas had run off with his wife. On Tuesday 17 February newspapers published a photograph of Mrs

Winkless, and Clapham landlady Mrs Smeed reported that the woman in the picture was lodging in her house with a young man. When Mrs Smeed took breakfast to their room Thomas answered the door and four policemen rushed at him as he dived for the bed, grabbing a gun from under the pillow. After a life or death struggle the officers overpowered Thomas, who said: 'That gun's full up and they were all for you, you bastards... You were lucky. I might just as well be hanged for a sheep as a lamb.' Thomas was sentenced to death but, due to an experimental five-year suspension of the death penalty, he was reprieved and his sentence commuted to life imprisonment. The murder of PC Edgar inspired the film *The Blue Lamp*, which in turn led to the hugely successful long-running TV series *Dixon of Dock Green*, starring Jack Warner.

☆ FIRST British defendant convicted of murder without a body

James Camb, Winchester Assizes. Monday 22 March 1948

In 1947, 21-year-old actress Gay Gibson was returning to London from Cape Town, South Africa, aboard SS *Durban Castle*. At 03:00 on 18 October, while the ship was approximately 90 miles off the West African coast, galley steward Frederick Steer answered a bell-push summons for Miss Gibson but on reaching her cabin the door was briefly opened by 31-year-old deck steward James Camb, who mumbled: 'It's all right.' The following morning Gibson was missing. Assuming she had fallen overboard, the ship turned about in a fruitless attempt to find her. Eventually, having been reluctant to shop a fellow crew member for consorting with guests, Steer reported the incident to the captain. Camb denied entering Gibson's cabin but agreed to a physical examination which revealed scratches on his shoulders and wrist which he claimed were heat rash. When the *Durban Castle* docked at Southampton

Camb changed his story, telling police that Gibson had greeted him wearing only a dressing gown and that she had died of a fit during consensual intercourse. He claimed to have tried artificial respiration and then panicked, pushing her body through the porthole. His trial opened at Winchester Assizes on 18 March 1948, and although there was no body the prosecution asked penetrating questions – if Gay had been naked when she met him why were her pyjamas missing? If it had been consensual sex why hadn't she used her diaphragm, which was found in her suitcase? Whose bloodstains, consistent with strangulation, were those on the bedsheet? The defence unwittingly helped the prosecution by revealing that there was urine on the sheet (overlooked by the pathologist Dr William Teare) which was in keeping with the act of strangulation, where victims often involuntarily discharge their bladder. Camb may have thought that without a body no charge could be brought but on 22 March the jury took just 45 minutes to find him guilty of murdering Gibson for rejecting his advances. He was sentenced to death but, because the Criminal Justice Bill's no-hanging clause was then being debated in parliament, he was reprieved. In 1967, eight years after being paroled, he was given probation for molesting a thirteen year old girl, and in 1969 he was returned to prison to serve out his complete life sentence after being convicted of more sexual offences against schoolgirls.

☆ FIRST FBI Most Wanted named

'Tough Tommy' Holden. Tuesday 14 March 1950

The famous list of the FBI's Ten Most Wanted Fugitives arose from a 1949 conversation between FBI Director J Edgar Hoover, and William Kinsey Hutchinson, editor-in-chief of the International News Service (the predecessor of the United Press International). Hoover and Hutchinson's discussion of ways to promote the capture of the FBI's 'toughest guys' resulted in an article, which received so much publicity that the list was born. The FBI's 'Most Wanted' programme officially began when Hoover named train robber and prison escapee 'Tough Tommy' Holden as No 1: he was sought for the 1949 murder of his wife and her two brothers at a Chicago drinking party. Nine days later, on 24 March, the first Top Ten was completed with the addition of another prison escapee, Morris Guralink, who had stabbed a girl for spurning his advances and then bitten off the arresting policeman's finger. Guralink was apprehended after a vicious struggle on 15 December 1950 while working in the Campus Clothes store in Madison, Wisconsin, and Holden was apprehended on 23 June 1951 in Breaverton, Oregon, where he was working as a plasterer.

DID YOU KNOW?

According to the FBI, the Most Wanted statistics are: age 36, height 5'9", weight 167 pounds; days on the list 157; apprehension 969 miles from crime scene. The shortest time on the list was two hours and the longest 18 years 4 months 9 days. Seven women have appeared on the list and some individuals have appeared twice. As of 19 October 2006, 484 fugitives have been listed and 454 captured or located, 148 (31%) of them due to public assistance. That works out at a success rate of 94%.

* LAST woman hanged in Australia

Jean Lee, Melbourne. 08:00 Monday 19 February 1951

After the failure of her marriage, red-head Jean Lee became a prostitute and con-woman, enticing men into compromising situations then having her pimp and lover Robert Clayton burst in as the outraged husband, demanding compensation (a ploy known in criminal slang as 'The Badger Game'). The couple later teamed up with petty criminal Norman Andrews, and on 7 November 1949 the trio targetted 73-year-old bookmaker William Kent in the University Hotel in Carlton, Melbourne. Having got him drunk, Lee enticed him back to the boarding house he owned at 50 Dorritt Street, where she began to steal his money. He struggled, so she smashed him over the head with an empty wine bottle and beat him with the leg of a chair that had broken during the struggle. Clayton and Andrews entered and ransacked the room searching for cash they were convinced Kent must have stashed away. Finding nothing, they tied his thumbs together with a bootlace and systematically tortured him for an hour by kicking him, slashing him with a penknife and burning him with lighted cigarettes. Finally Lee rammed the stub of the broken bottle in his face and they left Kent tied up, either dead or dying of suffocation. Being well known to the police they were soon arrested, and when found guilty Lee collapsed, crying, 'I didn't do it. I didn't do it.' For her execution in Melbourne's Pentridge Prison she had to be sedated, after which she was carried comatose to the scaffold and seated in a chair on the trapdoor before the final drop. Two hours later Clayton and Andrews were hanged side by side on the same gallows.

✱ LAST woman executed in Canada

Marguerite Pitre, Bordeaux Jail, Canada. Wednesday 8 July 1953

Canada's worst mass murderer was the lynchpin of a plot which took the lives of 23 people in order to ensure the death of one intended victim. The plot was the brainchild of Quebec jeweller J Albert Guay, who wanted rid of his wife Rita in order to obtain a hefty insurance payout and marry his new mistress, Marie-Ange Robitaille. Guay offered to cancel all of his former mistress Margueritte Pitre's loans if she delivered a timebomb to Quebec's

Ancienne-Lorette Airport, as well as handsomely paying her crippled brother, watchmaker Genereaux Ruest, to build the bomb. On 9 September 1949 a Quebec Airlines DC-3 exploded forty miles from Quebec in Canada's worst plane crash to that date. Investigators quickly established that a bomb had caused the disaster and discovered that one package was being sent to a non-existent address. Freight handlers remembered a woman in black leaving a 28lb (13kg) package officially recorded as 'religious statuary', and a taxi driver led police to the Pitre's address where they learned that she was in hospital recovering from a suicide attempt. When police arrived at the hospital her first words were: 'He made me do it.' All three conspirators were hanged, Ruest being taken to the scaffold in his wheelchair.

☆ FIRST British murderer hunted with the aid of television

William Pettit, BBC Television. Thursday 1 October 1953

'These are the pictures of William Pettit. The police are anxious to trace this man, who, it is believed, may assist inquiries into the death of Mrs Rene Brown at Chislehurst on 10 September'. This historic first TV appeal was made by the BBC's chief radio announcer John Snagge, who had been preferred over television duty announcer Sylvia Peters because the powers that be felt it would be more 'suitable' for a man to read such a serious messsage. Twenty-seven-year-old Pettit, who suffered from tuberculosis and had a long history of mental problems, had stabbed his mistress and former landlady, 48-year-old Mrs Agnes 'Rene' Brown, in a field by a path named Lover's Lane in Chislehurst, Kent. Weeks of intensive searching had failed to find Pettit, and TV executives agreed to transmit his picture to their 8 million viewers. Thus he became the most publicised and most elusive man in Britain.

Eventually, on 23 October, his corpse was found on a bomb site near Cannon Street Station in London. In his hand was a note written to his lover's husband, Arthur Brown: 'Forgive me for what I have done. I could have gone on living with Mr and Mrs Brown, but not without Mrs Brown. I love her, I love her, I love her.' According to pathologist Keith Simpson, Pettit had not committed suicide – he had died four or five weeks earlier, probably from advanced tuberculosis. On 27 August 1954 the bereaved Arthur Brown won a third dividend on the football pools, having said that he would continue to fill in his coupons in the hope that 'It might help me keep my mind off this terrible business.'

* LAST hanging in the Irish Republic

Michael Manning, Mountjoy Prison, Dublin. 08:00 Tuesday 20 April 1954

Manning, a 25-year-old labourer from Newcastle, near Limerick, hanged for the murder 65-year-old nun Catherine Cooper. Manning dragged Sister Cooper onto a golf course and brutally raped her after stuffing grass into her mouth to silence her screams – she actually died from suffocation caused by the grass. Manning was the 29th and last person hanged for non-political murder in the Irish Republic since its creation in 1922.

* LAST side-by-side double hanging in Britain

Kenneth Gilbert and Ian Grant, Pentonville Prison, London. Thursday 17 June 1954

Hotel workers Gilbert and Grant, 22 and 24, were convicted of murdering 55-year-old night porter George Smart on 9 March 1954 at the Aban Court Hotel in Kensington, London. After breaking in via the coal hole (a route Gilbert knew, having worked at the hotel) they intended to tie and gag the night porter and put him in the telephone kiosk. But Smart saw them and cornered Grant, who hit him; then Gilbert also struck him, breaking his jaw. The burglars then bound Smart and gagged him with a crepe bandage which slipped, so they added a serviette before grabbing what they could (£2 in cash and £7-worth of cigarettes) and leaving. Smart struggled to his feet but slipped and banged his nose which began bleeding and, because the gag made it impossible to breathe through his mouth, he quickly suffocated. Gilbert and Grant were caught after Grant bragged about the robbery to a friend who informed the police. At their trial they blamed each other but assured the jury that they never intended to kill Mr Smart. Recently the Crown prosecutor and both defence barristers (who at the time were only juniors because legal aid authorities refused to pay for leading defence counsel) have agreed there was a miscarriage of justice and that neither man should have hanged. Their appeals were not helped by the fact they were heard by Lord Goddard, the Lord Chief Justice, who was not only a strong believer in capital punishment but also lived close to the Aban Court Hotel and had been burgled himself only the previous year.

❏ ONLY Test cricketer to have been executed

Leslie Hylton, St Catherine's Prison, Jamaica. Tuesday 17 May 1955

Wisden's obituary of West Indies fast bowler Leslie G Hylton makes no mention of the nature of his demise, stating merely that he 'died in Jamaica on May 17, 1955, aged 50.' But Hylton didn't simply die; he was hanged for the murder of his wife Lurlene. The previous year Lurlene had confessed to adultery with notorious womaniser Roy Francis, telling Hylton: 'I'm in love with Roy. My body belongs to him,' and pulling up her nightdress as if to prove it. Hylton shot her seven times and then phoned the police. His defence counsel, Jamaican cricket captain Noel 'Crab' Nethersole, claimed that Hylton was attempting to shoot himself but missed. Lack of accuracy was not the most credible defence for a former Test bowler with an average of 26.6, particularly given that he would have had to stop to reload his revolver, but it still took the all-male jury fully ninety minutes to convict. While in the death cell he was received into the Roman Catholic Church.

✳ LAST woman executed in Britain

Ruth Ellis, Holloway Prison, London, England. 09:00 Wednesday 13 July 1955

On 10 April 1955, former model and club hostess Ruth Ellis shot her lover David Blakely four times outside The Magnolia pub in Hampstead, London. On being sentenced to death she simply said, 'Thanks.' Ellis spent just 23 days in the condemned cell before becoming executioner Albert Pierrepoint's sixteenth and last female client. Five minutes before the allotted time a telephoned reprieve offered a brief glimmer of hope for Ellis, but proved to be a hoax. She drank a large tot of brandy and set off for the scaffold where, Pierrepoint claimed, she pursed her lips as he hooded her, in the same provocative manner she had done when she was modelling for the Camera Club. Years later Pierrepoint said that she was 'the bravest woman I ever hanged', and at 28 she was also the youngest woman hanged in twentieth century Britain. Pierrepoint was paid 15 guineas for the execution, which is thought to have been a turning point in his views on capital punishment: 'I do not now believe that any one of the hundreds of executions I carried out has in any way acted as a deterrent against future murder. Capital punishment, in my view, achieved nothing except revenge.'

DID YOU KNOW?

The last two women to hang in Britain – Ruth Ellis (*left*) and Styllou Christofi, who killed on 29 July 1954 and was hanged on 15 December 1954 – both killed out of jealousy, both murdered their victims on South Hill Park Road, Hampstead, and were both hanged by Albert Pierrepoint.

✳ LAST execution by Albert Pierrepoint

Norman Green, Liverpool Prison. Wednesday 27 July 1955

Pierrepoint didn't know that the execution of 25-year-old Green would be his last. At Green's trial for the motiveless stabbing of ten-year-old Norman Yates he also confessed to fatally stabbing eleven-year-old William Harmer nine months earlier, and Pierrepoint duly dispatched him in July 1955. Pierrepoint's next assignment was scheduled for January 1956 but the convict was belatedly reprieved; Pierrepoint asked the Home Office for expenses towards his preparations but considered their offer so derisory that he resigned, making Green his last victim. In a 23-year career Pierrepoint was involved in some 435 hangings. His retirement marked the end of 55 years of the Pierrepoint dynasty during which Albert, his father, Henry, and his uncle, Tom, hanged more than 830 people.

☆ FIRST 'noddy bikes'

Metropolitan Police, London, England. Monday 19 September 1955

The lightweight Velocette with a water-cooled quiet engine made these bikes ideal for night duty patrols. The nickname derived from the fact while riding officers couldn't take their hands off the handlebars to salute inspectors, so instead they nodded.

☆ FIRST use in England of bare footprints as evidence

Sydney Malkin, Hastings. Tuesday 1 May 1956

Malkin, a 47-year-old chef, was charged with breaking and entering a flat and stealing nylon panties and a slip valued at £2. The owner, Mrs Edith Mary Bowles, had left the garments on her mantelpiece to dry before going to bed but, as her flat was sixty feet above the ground, she hadn't locked her windows. While investigating this unlikely theft, PC Ernest Parker found the imprint of a bare right foot on top of the television, the imprint of a left foot on the floor, and a further footprint on a loudspeaker cabinet. At Malkin's trial Detective Superintendent Holten of Scotland Yard's fingerprint department stated that whilst this was the first time footprint evidence had been used in England, where people usually wear shoes, 'The system is used widely in countries where people go barefooted such as Africa, India, Ceylon.'

☆ FIRST surveillance camera

St Clair Savings and Loan, Cleveland, Ohio. spring 1957

The 16mm movie camera proved an almost instant success when, during its first year in operation, pictures taken during a raid led to the capture of the three culprits within 36 hours.

✳ LAST man hanged in New Zealand

Walter Bolton, Auckland. Monday 18 February 1957

Beatrice Mabel Bolton (née Jones) died on 11 July 1955 after a long and debilitating illness which a post mortem revealed to have been caused by arsenic poisoning. Walter, her husband of 42 years, was a sheep farmer, and police at first thought that arsenic from his sheep dips must have entered Beatrice's system accidentally in small amounts. Then it was discovered that 68-year-old Walter had been enjoying an affair with his wife's widowed sister, Florence, who nursed Beatrice through her final illness. Bolton was put on trial and, despite lack of evidence, was condemned to death for murder – his hanging at Mount Eden Prison was botched and he slowly strangled to death, after which Florence committed suicide. In 2001 his son James Bolton shocked New Zealand by claiming that his father was innocent and that Florence had murdered Beatrice, saying that she had killed other people before.

❏ ONLY accused in Britain to claim amnesia as a defence against a capital offence
✳ LAST person to be hanged in Britain for the murder of a police officer

Gunther Fritz Podola, Wandsworth Prison. 09:45 Thursday 5 November 1959

In 1959, having been deported from Canada for theft and burglary, German-born Podola arrived in Britain where he called himself Mike Colato. On 3 July that year he burgled the South Kensington flat of an American model, Mrs Verne Schiffman, stealing jewellery and furs worth £2,000 and trying to blackmail his victim by claiming to have embarrassing photos and tape recordings of her. Knowing she had nothing to hide Schiffman told police, who tapped her line and traced Podola's next call to a public telephone inside South Kensington underground station. Two unarmed detectives, John Sandford and Raymond Purdy, moved in and arrested him but Podola twisted free. Sandford and

Purdy cornered him in a block of flats at 105 Onslow Square, where Podola suddenly produced a 9mm FB Radom V15 pistol, shot Purdy through the heart, and again escaped. When Purdy's belongings were returned to his widow she discovered Podola's address book, which Purdy had taken when first arresting him. This led police to the Claremont House Hotel in Kensington. On 16 July armed police assembled outside room 15, where Podola was staying, and shouted, 'Police! Open this door!' Hearing a click like the cocking of a gun, 16.5 stone Sergeant Chambers charged the door and Podola, who must have been listening on the other side, was floored, landing with his head in the fireplace. He was hospitalised for four days as a result, and claimed to have lost his memory of everything up to 17 July. At his Old Bailey trial it was proved that he had shot Purdy, but if he genuinely couldn't recall doing so he would have been acquitted. The jury rejected Podola's defence and his lawyer, Frederick Lawton, thought there were no grounds for appeal – but the Home Secretary made legal history by sending the case to the Court of Appeal as if it had been referred by the defence. The appeal was rejected and Podola was hanged by Harry Allen. Purdy's widow, with three children to support, received an annual pension of £546.

☆ FIRST white man hanged for murder of black person in Kenya

Peter Poole, Nairobi, Kenya. Thursday 18 August 1960

Poole, a 28 year-old Essex-born engineer, was executed for shooting a black servant who had been throwing stones at his dog. His defence team tried to prove he had become mentally unstable after fighting with British forces against the Mau Mau. To the end Poole was convinced he would not hang because he had 'only killed a black man'.

☆ FIRST murderer caught by Identikit
✳ LAST man hanged at Pentonville Prison

Edwin Albert Bush, Old Compton Street, Soho, London. Wednesday 8 March 1961

On 3 March 1961, hoping to raise £10 to buy an engagement ring for his girlfriend, Bush robbed and killed shopkeeper Elsie Batten. After battering her with a stone vase and stabbing her with two antique daggers, he stole a ceremonial sword from the London antiques shop where she worked; Elsie was found with one antique dagger protruding from her chest and another from her neck. Instead of the usual artist's impression of the wanted man police issued an 'Identikit' picture composed of facial features approved by three witnesses from a selection of different hairlines, foreheads, eye-brows, eyes, cheeks, noses, lips, chins and necks. This system was introduced from the US where it had been invented by Sheriff Hugh MacDonald of Los Angeles. It proved so accurate that five days later Bush was arrested in Old Compton Street, a short walk from the scene of the crime. Pakistani-born Bush, 21, sought to use racism as his defence, claiming that he had lost his temper when Mrs Batten had said, 'You niggers are all the same. You come in and never buy anything.' The Old Bailey jury was unimpressed and Bush duly became the last man to hang at Pentonville. During the 1970s Identikit was superseded by Photofit.

☆ FIRST skyjacking in America

Antulio Ramirez Ortiz, Marathon, Florida. Monday 1 May 1961

On 1 May 1961 Ortiz, a 34-year-old Puerto Rican, boarded National Airlines Flight 337 with six other passengers for the flight from Marathon, Florida, to Key West. Once airborne Ortiz, brandishing a revolver and knife, ordered co-pilot JT Richardson out of his seat; he then occupied the co-pilot's seat and ordered Captain Francis Riley to change course for Havana, Cuba. Ortiz told Riley that he had been offered $100,000 by General Rafael Trujillo Molina of the Dominican Republic to kill Fidel Castro, but after a change of heart he wanted to warn Castro of the plot against him. On arrival at Havana Ortiz was taken into custody by Cuban authorities, who allowed the plane and its passengers to continue with their journey, and on 28 July 1961 a grand jury in Florida indicted Ortiz in absentia. However, it wasn't until 11 November 1975, fully fourteen years after the historic first skyjacking, that Ortiz was finally arrested by FBI agents in Miami. He was convicted of air piracy and sentenced to twenty years in prison.

❑ ONLY person executed in Israel

Adolf Eichmann, Ramleh Prison, Tel Aviv, Israel. 23:58 Thursday 31 May 1962

Eichmann was the mastermind behind Hitler's *Endlosung* – 'Final Solution' – which resulted in the extermination of six million Jews. It was he who determined in what order, in what countries and by what methods the Jews were to die. After the war Eichmann escaped to Argentina but fifteen years later, on the evening of 11 May 1960, seven men in two cars pulled over in front of a house in Garibaldi Street, Buenos Aires. One of the cars had apparently broken down and five of the men hovered around discussing the best way to repair it. Then the owner of the house, 'Ricardo Klement', arrived home. In a flash he was grabbed by the men, who were agents of the Israeli secret service Mossad, and then smuggled out of Argentina. His trial began on 11 April 1961 in the courtroom of the newly built Beth Ha'am, or 'House of the People', in Jerusalem. He heard the evidence from inside a bulletproof glass cage big enough to hold him and two guards. When he defended himself as 'only a minor transport officer', guilty only of having deported Jews, he was reminded of his boast: 'I will leap to my grave laughing because the feeling that I have five million human beings on my conscience is for me a source of extraordinary satisfaction.' The fourteen-week trial examined 1,500 documents and heard the testimony of 100 prosecution witnesses, including 90 who had survived the horrors of the concentration camps. The three judges spent four months deliberating on their decision: Eichmann was to hang. On the scaffold he told the assembled witnesses they would all soon meet again and that he died believing in God. 'Long live Germany... Argentina... Austria... I greet my wife, my family and my friends. I had to obey the rules of war and my flag.' He refused the black hood, and the noose was placed around his neck. Three men screened by blankets (one of whom was the English executioner Harry Allen) each pulled a lever; one was a dummy and the other two released the bolts that held the trapdoor. The body was cremated and before dawn the following morning a police boat carried his ashes beyond the Israeli three-mile limit and scattered them in international waters. One wonders if on the scaffold Eichmann recognised the ultimate proof of his failure – both his trial and execution took place in a Jewish country that had not existed when his crimes were committed. Ironically, as a child the dark-complexioned Eichmann was frequently mistaken for a Jew.

✱ LAST prisoner of Alcatraz

Frank C Weatherman, San Francisco Bay. Thursday 21 March 1963

For 29 notorious years Alcatraz stood as a grim icon of judicial revenge. It was the toughest of all US federal institutions, with strictly enforced rules of silence and total obedience, and boasted that it was escape-proof, being separated from the mainland by a narrow strait of freezing shark-infested water swept by deadly currents. Many inmates were internationally known, including Al Capone and Robert Stroud, 'The Birdman of Alcatraz'. (Actually Stroud kept canaries while at Leavenworth Penitentiary but never kept any in Alcatraz, so he should really be known as 'Birdman of Leavenworth'.) Alcatraz witnessed five suicides and eight murders but no executions. Although there were 336 cells the average number of prisoners was only 260 with the maximum of 302. The average time spent on the island was eight to ten years. On 21 March 1963 Warden Blackwell lined up the last 27 inmates and marched them silently in single file down the main corridor and out to the prison launch to take them to the mainland. Appropriately, the last inmate to be incarcerated was also the last to board the boat – Frank C Weatherman, #AZ-1576. Although Alcatraz housed a total of 1,546 inmates, Weatherman's number was 1,576 because 28 inmates received two numbers by serving separate prison terms. Theodore 'Blackie' Audett is the only prisoner to have been issued with three separate numbers. Asked how he felt about the closure of the institution, Weatherman gave the perfect eulogy: 'Alcatraz was never good for anybody.'

DID YOU KNOW?

Alcatraz Island is named after the birds that proliferated there – *Isla de Alcatraces* means 'Island of Pelicans' – but it later became known by its more forbidding name: The Rock. The facility on the tiny island started with a lighthouse in 1854 (the first on the Pacific Coast), then a military prison from 1859 until 1933. The military left 32 tough prisoners who were immediately assigned Alcatraz numbers alphabetically, Frank Bolt becoming #AZ-01. On 13 July 1934 Frederick Grant Wright became the first civilian inmate. Coincidentally the second civilian inmate, forger Robert Bradford Moxon, had once served on Alcatraz as a soldier.

✽ LAST execution in Scotland

Henry John Burnett, Craiginches Prison, Aberdeen. 08:00 Thursday 15 August 1963

Burnett, 21, was living with 24-year-old mother-of-two Margaret Guyan who was estranged from her husband Thomas Guyan. Burnett, who had a history of mental instability, became so possessive that he would lock Margaret in the house when he went out. Things became so bad that Margaret decided to return to Thomas but on 31 May 1963, while gathering her possessions, Burnett held a knife to her throat and threatened to kill her. Margaret fled to the safety of her husband's house and Burnett followed – going first to his get brother's shotgun. Burnett burst into the Guyans' house and as Thomas opened the kitchen door Burnett gave him both barrels in the face. He then grabbed Margaret, dragged her to a local garage and stole a car at gunpoint. When police gave chase Burnett, realising the futility of running, quietly gave himself up. His two-day trial opened on 23 July at Aberdeen High Court, where his defence counsel claimed it was a clear case of insanity, revealing he had been violent in the past and had attempted suicide. But after only 25 minutes the jury found him guilty of murder. After he was sentenced both his own family and the Guyans petitioned for his reprieve despite which, on 15 August, Burnett became Scotland's last victim of the rope.

☆ FIRST murder transmitted on live television

Jack Ruby, Police HQ, Dallas, Texas. 12:21 Sunday 24 November 1963

Two days after the assassination of US President John F Kennedy live news bulletins showed the prime suspect, Lee Harvey Oswald, being transferred from Dallas Police HQ to nearby Dallas County

Jail. Oswald was handcuffed to plainclothes Detective Leavelle and at 11:21, as they walked through the basement towards the transfer vehicle, nightclub owner Jack Ruby stepped forward and fired a single shot from a snub-nosed Colt Cobra .38, yelling 'You killed my President, you rat!' Oswald was rushed to the same hospital where JFK had died but the doctors – two of whom had attempted to save Kennedy – were unable to save him. At 13:07, exactly 47 hours and 53 minutes after Kennedy died, Oswald too was pronounced dead. On 14 March 1964 Ruby was convicted of murder with malice, for which he received a death sentence – then, in November 1966, the conviction and death sentence were overturned. Arrangements were being made for a second trial when, on 3 January 1967, Ruby died of a pulmonary embolism at Dallas's Parkland Memorial Hospital – which meant that the president, the alleged assassin and the alleged assassin's murderer all died in the same place.

✻ LAST men hanged in Britain (for murder)

Gwynne Owen Evans, Strangeways Prison, Manchester, and Peter Anthony Allen, Walton Jail, Liverpool. 08:00 Thursday 13 August 1964

There was no single last person hanged in Britain – Allen and Evans (real name John Robson Walby), aged 21 and 24, were hanged at the same time on the same day for a murder they both denied committing. By coincidence Britain's last chief hangman was also called Allen, and the middle name of the murder victim was Alan. On 7 April 1964, 52-year-old John Alan West was stabbed to death during a robbery at his home near Workington, Cumberland. Among items found at the scene were an off-white raincoat containing a wallet with the name and address of 'Miss Mary O'Brien', and a Royal Life-Saving Medallion inscribed 'G O Evans July 1961.' Within 48 hours police picked up Allen, who was married to Mary, née O'Brien, and his lodger Evans, who was a known acquaintance of West. Both confessed to the robbery but each implicated the other as the murderer – although Evans made a classic blunder, saying, 'I don't know anything about a knife. I don't have to use a knife to kill a man. I'm an expert at judo and karate.' Police hadn't mentioned a knife, and Evans thus put his own neck in the noose. Double executions had long since ceased, so Allen and Evans were taken to separate prisons. Mary Allen took their two children to visit Allen the day before his execution, which was his baby son's first birthday. Allen went berserk, breaking his wrist and finger against the bullet-proof glass of the visiting room. He was hanged in Liverpool by Robert Leslie Stewart at the same moment as Evans was hanged in Manchester by Harry Allen. Thus ended capital punishment in Britain, this rare pair of hangings bringing the total of British hangings in the twentieth century to 817.

✻ LAST person executed in South Australia

Glen Valance, Adelaide, South Australia. Tuesday 24 November 1964

After being sacked from his job at Kooroon Station, 23-year-old farm worker Valance went on the rampage, tying up three fellow workers and shooting his erstwhile boss, farmer Richard Strang, as he lay sleeping. He then raped Mrs Strang in the bed next to her husband's corpse. His plea of insanity was rejected and a masked hangman executed him in Adelaide Prison's notorious 'Hanging Tower'.

☆ FIRST criminal caught by satellite

George Lemay, Fort Lauderdale, Florida. Sunday 2 May 1965

On 1 July 1961 Montreal-born playboy George Lemay masterminded one of the biggest heists in Canadian history. The 35-year-old controlled the robbery by walkie-talkie from outside the Montreal branch of the Bank of Nova Scotia as his gang blasted an 18-inch hole in the concrete floor of the vault, rifled through 377 safety deposit boxes, and escaped with more than $630,000; a record haul at that time. The following year five of his accomplices were arrested but Lemay had disappeared. Then, on 2 May 1965 his photo was transmitted across Europe, Canada and United States using Early Bird, the first commercial communications satellite, in an test exchange of 'Wanted' persons between Scotland Yard, the FBI and the RCMP. A boatyard worker at Fort Lauderdale immediately recognised Lemay as the owner of the sloop *Tirana*. The owner insisted that he was Rene Roy but fingerprints proved him to be Lemay, who boasted: 'It took a satellite to catch me!' and offered to sell his sloop to police for a bargain price, joking that he wouldn't be using it for a while. While in the 'escape proof' Dade County Jail, Miami, Lemay shrewdly married the only witness against him and even managed to enjoy a honeymoon, escaping by tying a radiator to a utilities cable and using it to slide ninety feet from the seventh floor before dropping the last fifteen feet to the ground where a waiting car drove him to freedom. He was recaptured eleven months later in the Golden Nugget Casino, Las Vegas, and returned to Canada where, on 17 January 1969, he was sentenced to eight years.

✳ LAST execution in Australia

Ronald Ryan, Pentridge Prison, Melbourne, Australia. 08:00 Friday 3 February 1967

On 19 December 1965 Ryan, serving nine years for burglary, and Peter Walker, serving twelve years for armed robbery, executed an audacious escape from Melbourne's Pentridge Prison. They were pursued by armed prison officers one of whom, 41-year-old George Hodson, managed to grab Walker – but as he did so, Ryan fatally shot him in the chest with a stolen prison carbine. Helped by accomplice Arthur Henderson, Ryan and Walker went on the run, financing their venture by robbery – including a bank robbery on the day of Hodson's funeral. On 27 December Henderson's corpse was found in a public lavatory, shot in the back of the head, and nine days later Ryan and Walker were arrested in Sydney. Walker was sentenced to twelve years for the manslaughter of Hodson and life for the manslaughter of Henderson, and Ryan was sentenced to death. There was tremendous opposition to the execution, including a 3,000-strong trade union march on Victoria's Parliament House in Melbourne. On the day, 300 policemen protected the prison from 3,000 people demonstrating against the hanging. Inside, the anonymous hangman – believed to be a retired prison officer – marched Ryan five paces from his cell to the trap door, which was set into the steel catwalk spanning the first floor galleries in the main central corridor of the cell block. In a letter not revealed until 1988 Ryan stated that he had aimed for Hodson's shoulder, but in the struggle with Walker Hodson had moved and taken the bullet in the chest. Ryan died on same gallows as Jean Lee, the last woman to be hanged in Australia, and there is strong evidence to suggest the same executioner hanged them both. Between 1819 (when the name Australia was first used) and 1967 there were 1,700 official executions in Australia.

☆ FIRST female addition to the FBI's Most Wanted list

Ruth Eisemann-Schier. Saturday 28 December 1968

On 17 December 1968 Eisemann-Schier and her lover, career criminal Gary Steven Krist, abducted twenty-year-old student Barbara Jane Mackle at gunpoint from the Rodeway Inn in Decatur, Georgia. They bound and chloroformed Barbara's mother and left her behind. Barbara was driven to a remote pine forest near Duluth and buried alive in a fibreglass box supplied with a battery-powered lamp, an air pump, 30,000 calories of food, five blankets, a foam rubber mattress, a pillow, and water laced with sedatives. They demanded $500,000 ransom from Barbara's father, Robert F Mackle, a millionaire Florida land developer and personal friend of president-elect Richard Nixon. The collection went awry when a policeman on routine patrol gave chase thinking Krist was a burglar, but Krist's abandoned vehicle rendered clues that led to both kidnappers being put on the Most Wanted list. On 20 December a phone-call revealed where Barbara was buried and, after 83 hours underground, she was exhumed alive and well. Eisemann-Schier and Krist had split up: Krist used the ransom money to buy a speedboat, but was spotted by a Coast Guard helicopter and arrested after a high-speed chase; Eisemann-Schier was apprehended on 5 March 1969 in Norman, Oklahoma. She was sentenced to seven years in prison, paroled after serving four years and then deported to her native Honduras where she now lives with her husband and four children. Krist was sentenced to life in 1969 but released on parole in 1979. Barbara is happily married with two children, and declines all requests for interviews.

☆ FIRST kidnap-and-ransom perpetrated in Britain

Arthur and Nizamodeen Hosein, Wimbledon, London. c 18:00 Monday 29 December 1969

Britain's first kidnap victim was the subject of mistaken identity. Trinidad-born brothers Arthur and Nizamodeen Hosein, 34 and 22, abducted Mrs Muriel McKay from her home at 20 Arthur Road, Wimbledon, believing her to be the wife of newspaper tycoon Rupert Murdoch. Asked whether police were sure the ransom demand was genuine, DSC Smith, who was leading the inquiry, replied: 'How do we know? We've never had one before.' Forty-one days later police raided Rooks Farm, the Hoseins' remote and dilapidated pig farm at Stocking Pelham in Hertfordshire, and arrested the two brothers. It transpired that Arthur, unable to make ends meet, had hatched the kidnap plot after seeing Murdoch interviewed on television by David Frost. Arthur was sentenced to 49 years and Nizamodeen to 39 years. Mrs McKay's body was never found, and it is thought that she was drugged, shot, butchered, and fed to the Hoseins' herd of Wessex saddleback pigs.

☆ FIRST use of Photofit
☆ FIRST Photofit transmitted on television

Police Five. *Sunday 22 November 1970*

In 1938, long before the invention of Identikit, Jacques Penry had been experimenting with building photographic montages from eyes, noses, mouths and chins. It took Penry 22 years to develop his montages into Photofit, and meanwhile Identikit was already being used (*see 1961*). On 14 October 1970 James William Camerton was found dead in his London bedroom. An Identikit picture was built from witness descriptions of a man seen loitering outside Camerton's home on 9 and 10 October, and on 16 October the composite picture was shown on the television programme *Police Five*. Presenter Shaw Taylor appealed for viewers' assistance and reminded fans, as always, to 'Keep 'em peeled'. Witnesses came forward and it was decided to build a better picture using Photofit. On 22 November the new picture was transmitted on *Police Five*, and a witness led police to arrest John Ernest Bennett at his home in Nottinghamshire, where the murder weapon and property stolen from the murder scene were recovered. Bennett was sentenced to life imprisonment. In 1988 Photofit was replaced by E-Fit (Electronic Facial Identification) which applied computer graphics to face-building exercises.

❏ ONLY kidnap attempt on a member of the British Royal Family

Princess Anne, The Mall, London, England. 19:45 Wednesday 20 March 1974

Princess Anne and her husband Captain Mark Phillips were returning to Buckingham Palace after attending a charity film show in aid of the Riding for the Disabled Association, of which Anne is patron. They were followed by a hired white Ford Escort driven by 26-year-old schizophrenic and petty criminal Ian Ball, who was armed with two Astra revolvers, a five-shot .38 and an eleven-shot .22, plus 58 spare rounds of ammunition, four sets of regulation handcuffs and a letter to the Queen. At 19:45, just after royal chauffeur Alec Callender had turned into The Mall, Ball overtook both Anne's limousine and a white mini that was already overtaking it, then swerved across both cars causing everyone to brake. Anne's personal protection officer, Inspector James Beaton (armed with a Walther PP automatic) leapt out of the car but Ball was already pointing his .38 revolver at Callender and saying: 'Switch off the ignition.' Ball then went to the rear window and said to Princess Anne: 'I want you to come with me for a day or two, because I want two million. Will you get out of the car?' The princess, who is famous for her down-to-earth plain speaking replied: 'Not bloody likely – and I haven't got two million.' Beaton approached Ball who fired twice, one bullet grazing Beaton's jacket, the second blasting into his shoulder and piercing his lung. Despite his injury Beaton tried to return fire but his first shot missed and then the Walther jammed. Callender then grabbed Ball from behind but Ball turned and fired a bullet into his chest from point-blank range. He then grabbed the princess by the forearm, saying 'Please get out' and telling Beaton, 'Drop that gun, or I'll shoot her.' As Ball attempted to pull Anne out of the car Mark held her round the waist. The princess calmly asked him why he wanted to take her and Ball said, 'I'll get a couple of a million.' Mark managed to close the door and as Ball raised his gun to fire Beaton put his hand over the muzzle, at which Ball shot him in the stomach. PC Michael Hills, who was on duty outside St James's Palace, ran to the scene, grabbed Ball by the elbow and said: 'What's going on?' Ball replied by shooting him in the stomach. Several passers-by got involved, including Fleet Street reporter Brian McConnell who approached Ball saying, 'You can't do that. These are my friends. Don't be silly. Just give me the gun.' Ball warned him, 'Keep out of this. Get back,' but McConnell stepped forward and Ball shot him in the chest. Another stranger, Ronald Russell, punched Ball on the side of his head – Ball responded with a bullet that missed. Russell attacked him again and Ball ran off but was rugby-tackled to the ground by trainee detective Peter Edmonds. In just seven minutes eleven shots had been fired and four people had been wounded. On 22 May Ball was tried at the Old Bailey pleading guilty to two charges of attempted murder, two of wounding, and one of 'attempting to steal and carry away Her Royal Highness Princess Anne'. The judge, Lord Chief Justice Widgery, ordered that Ball be detained under the Mental Health Act 'without limit of time'. Beaton was awarded the George Cross, Britain's highest honour for peacetime gallantry. Russell and PC Hills were awarded the George Medal. Callender, Edmonds and McConnell all won the Queen's Gallantry Medal. All the policemen involved wear a special tie with a motif including a coronet, crossed pistols and a ball. Later Anne revealed: 'I nearly lost my temper with him, but I knew that if I did, I should hit him and he would shoot me.' The Duke of Edinburgh is alleged to have said that Ball was lucky to have failed because had Anne been taken 'she would have given him a hell of a time in captivity.'

☆ FIRST female African-American police officer killed in the line of duty

Gail A Cobb, Washington, DC, Friday 20 September 1974

Cobb, a 24-year-old first-year officer with the Metropolitan Police Department in Washington, DC, was walking her beat when she was tipped off that a suspected bank robber, John Willie Bryant, had just fled into a nearby underground garage. She surprised Bryant as he came out of a toilet, and ordered him to place his hands against the wall. As she radioed for assistance Bryant turned and fired a single shot at point-blank range, the bullet passing through her wrist and her police radio before penetrating her heart – she died at the scene. Cobb was killed in the deadliest year in US law enforcement history: in 1974 a total of 271 federal, state and local law enforcers were killed in the line of duty. The 1970s as a whole was the deadliest decade in US police history, with an average of 222 officer fatalities each year.

☆ FIRST serial sex killers in Ireland start their campaign of terror

John Shaw and Geoffrey Evans, Brittas Bay, Co. Wicklow, Ireland. Saturday 28 August 1976

Englishmen Shaw and Evans kidnapped and killed their first victim, 23-year-old Elizabeth Plunkett, on Saturday 28 August 1976, and her body was found 32 days later trussed up in Brittas Bay. By then the men had already claimed their second victim, 25-year-old Mary Duffy, a part-time cook from Belcarra, Co. Mayo. Duffy had been working a late-night shift at a Castlebar coffee shop when Evans and Shaw drove up alongside her and threw her into their vehicle before drugging her and taking her to a Galway caravan park where they held her captive and repeatedly raped her. Finally they smothered her, weighed her body down with an anchor, a block of cement and sledgehammer, and dumped it in Lough Inagh. In February 1978 Shaw, 32, was sentenced to life imprisonment for Duffy's murder plus fourteen years for rape and two years for false imprisonment. Evans, 34, was sentenced to life for Duffy's murder plus twenty years for the rape of both women. Shaw told the detectives, 'God help me. It was the Devil made me do it.'

* LAST guillotining in France

Hamida Djandoubi (Djarioubi), Baumetes Prison, Marseilles, France. 04:40 Saturday 10 September 1977

Tunisian immigrant Djandoubi moved to Marseille in 1968 and worked there as a packer until 1971, when he lost two-thirds of his right leg in a workplace accident. Two years later his lover, 21-year-old Elisabeth Bousquet, filed a complaint against him for illegal confinement and cruelty, claiming that he had tried to force her into prostitution. After his arrest and eventual release from custody Djandoubi started as a pimp with two new young girls. In July 1974, still wanting revenge on Bousquet, he kidnapped her and took her to his home where, in front of the terrified girls, he beat her unmercifully before burning her breasts and genitals with a cigarette. Bousquet survived the attack but Djandoubi took her by car to the outskirts of Marseille and strangled her. A month later two children discovered her body. Eventually, on 24 February 1974, Djandoubi was tried in Aix-en-Provence for torture, murder, rape and premeditated violence. He claimed that the effects of the amputation of his leg had turned him into a 'different' man. On 25 February he was condemned to death, but the appeal process meant that Djandoubi 's decapitation, carried out by executioner Marcel Chevalier, was delayed for a further three years.

☆ FIRST murder of a federal judge in America

Charles V Harrelson, San Antonio, Texas. Tuesday 29 May 1979

Harrelson, a professional card player, served ten years in Fort Leavenworth for the $2,000 contract killing of Texas grain dealer Sam Dedelia. On his release he was offered a reputed $250,000 to kill Judge John H Wood, who was known as 'Maximum John' because of his policy when sentencing guilty felons. Harrelson was caught after one of the biggest-ever FBI manhunts, and when Judge William Session sentenced him to a double life term he described him as 'the most vicious, heartless, cold-blooded killer I have come across'. Harrelson is the father of the actor Woody Harrelson.

☆ FIRST to die by lethal injection

Charles Brooks Jnr, Huntsville Prison, Texas. 00:09 Tuesday 7 December 1982

In 1977 Oklahoma became the first state to legislate for lethal injection; Texas followed suit later the same year and carried out the world's first execution by this method on 7 December 1982, when 40-year-old negro Charles Brooks was put to death for the murder of second-hand car salesman David Gregory on 14 December 1976 in Huntsville, Texas. While on death row Brooks converted to Islam, and in the death cell he went through a brief ritual concluding with the words, 'May Allah admit you to Paradise'. At Brooks's request his girlfriend, Vanessa Sapp, witnessed the entire procedure, which began at 00:09. Because of ethical problems of a physician deliberately causing death, the lethal dose was administered by a medical technician – it comprised a mixture of sodium thiopental (aka sodium pentothal, the 'truth drug'), pancuronium bromide (aka Pavulon, a muscle relaxant), and potassium chloride. Brooks, whose arm was decorated with a tattoo reading 'I was born to die', seemed to die quite easily. After the injection he raised his head, clenched his fist and seemed to yawn or gasp before passing into unconsciousness. He was pronounced dead at 00.16. Outside the prison one supporter of the death penalty complained, 'It's too lenient. They've got to go out painfully.'

❏ ONLY mass-escape from America's death row

The Mecklenburg Six, Mecklenburg Correctional Center, Boydton, Virginia. 22:47 Thursday 31 May 1984

Opened in March 1977 at a cost of $20 million, Virginia's 360-inmate Mecklenberg Correctional Center was a facility for the 'worst of the worst' and was known as a 'monument to failure'. In 1984 convicts on death row hatched a daring escape plan which involved most of the inmates and led to the escape of 'the Mecklenberg Six': brothers James and Linwood Briley, who had committed at least eleven murders between them; Lem Davis Tuggle, the only white inmate, who had raped and murdered two women; double murderer Earl Clanton; Derick Peterson, who had shot a man during a robbery; and Willie Jones who had murdered a friend's parents. At 20:00 on 31 May prisoners returning from the exercise yard bunched together when the electric gates opened and all jostled forward, making it impossible to count them properly, and in the confusion Clanton slipped into the bathroom. Over the next hour two makeshift knives were distributed to each of the six escapees and at 21:00 Peterson pressed his blade against a guard's throat, telling him not to make a sound. Meanwhile Briley asked the control booth guard to pass a paperback book to a fellow inmate on the other side of the block. The moment the guard opened the door Clanton burst from his hiding place and took over the control room. He opened all the cell doors and the prisoners quickly overpowered the guards, ordering them to strip to their underwear and tying their hands behind their backs. The prisoners quickly dressed in the uniforms, and as fresh guards arrived for their shifts they were quickly overpowered, until by 22:00 the prisoners had a dozen hostages. They forced one of the guards to phone the main control room, saying they had found an unexploded bomb and needed a van parked by the entrance to the death row to remove it to a safe distance. The six escapees, in guards' uniforms, then took over the main control room, located the riot gear and grabbed helmets and shields. Next they covered a television with a blanket, placed it on a stretcher and carried it out to the waiting van, Linwood spraying the 'bomb' with a fire extinguisher. Five piled into the back and Linwood jumped into the driver's seat, radioing the tower to open the gates. They drove out of the prison at 22:47. Clanton and Peterson were caught the following day, both drunk in a laundromat, still wearing what appeared to be the warders' shirts with the badges ripped off. Tuggle and Jones made it to Vermont but Tuggle was apprehended on 8 June after robbing a souvenir shop for petrol money. Guessing that something had gone wrong with Tuggle's financial expedition, Jones telephoned his mother who begged him to surrender; he gave himself up the same day, just five miles south of the Canadian border. The Brileys reached Philadelphia where James became 'Slim' and Linwood 'Lucky'. Their uncle arranged for them to work as handymen in Dan's Custom Car Factory but he was already under surveillance and the brothers were apprehended on 19 June in an FBI swoop. And so the last of the Mecklenberg Six were captured just nineteen days after their historic escape. None escaped execution. Linwood Briley was executed on 12 October 1984, James Briley on 18 April 1985, Clanton on 14 April 1988, Peterson on 22 August 1991, Jones on 15 September 1992 and Tuggle on 12 December 1996.

☆ **FIRST** American citizen deported for war crimes

Valerian Trifa, Green Lake Michigan. Tuesday 14 August 1984

On 17 July 1950 Viorel Trifa, a 36-year-old Romanian-born priest, entered the USA. After hearing about his ordeal in Nazi concentration camps immigration officials granted him residency; by 1952 he was a bishop and had adopted the name Valerian; and in 1957 he was naturalised a US citizen. Meanwhile, it was rumoured that Trifa had been one of the leaders of Romania's pro-Nazi Iron Guard, which massacred almost 6,000 people over three days in January 1941, and that when the public turned against the Iron Guard Trifa had fled to Germany. Trifa strenuously denied the rumours, and by 1975 he had been elevated to archbishop. But in May 1982 the West German government handed over the Trifa files, including a postcard dated 14 June 1942, apparently from Trifa to Heinrich Himmler, head of the Nazi SS. Trifa denied having written it but the FBI fingerprint department, using argon laser technology, detected the latent impression of a left thumbprint. Trifa's was an exact match, and on 14 August 1984 'Valerian' Trifa was deported to Portugal. Was it a coincidence or a missed clue that 21 January, the date of the Iron Guard massacre, is also the Feast Day of St Valerian?

☆ **FIRST** woman executed by lethal injection
✳ **LAST** woman executed in North Carolina

Margi Velma Barfield, Central Prison, Raleigh, North Carolina. 02:00 Friday 2 November 1984

Barfield, a 52-year-old nurse's aide, was convicted of poisoning her fiancé by lacing his iced tea with ant and cockroach poison. She also admitted using arsenic to poison one husband, her mother, and two invalids she had been attending, the motive for most of the killings being to stop the victims discovering that she had stolen money from them to buy drugs. Being the first woman to be executed in the US for 22 years many people fought for a reprieve, including evangelist Billy Graham's wife and daughter, who claimed that during her imprisonment Barfield had become a born-again Christian. But the appeal process failed, and for her execution Barfield wore pink floral-print pyjamas and blue slippers over the regulation prison-supplied diaper (necessary because the anal sphincter relaxes at death, often causing the bowel to release it contents). Matrons from another prison strapped Barfield to the death gurney because Central's own matrons had grown too fond of her to assist in the execution. Three syringes were attached to intravenous tubes through a curtain. Three executioners simultaneously depressed the plungers but only two were connected to Barfield so none of the volunteer executioners knew which of them had killed her. The injections were a mixture of sodium thiopental (aka sodium pentothal), pancuronium bromide and potassium chloride. She was pronounced dead at 02:15, after which her corpse rushed to hospital as she had offered to donate her liver, kidneys and eyes for transplant. Ultimately her bone, skin and eyes were used.

☆ FIRST criminal case decided by DNA evidence

Richard Buckland, Leicester. Friday 21 November 1986

Remarkably, the first time DNA decided a case it established innocence rather than guilt. So-called 'genetic fingerprinting', a system perfected by Professor (now Sir) Alec Jeffreys of Leicester University, secured the acquittal of Richard Buckland, a seventeen-year-old kitchen porter from Narborough, Leicestershire, who had confessed to murdering fifteen-year-old Dawn Ashworth on 31 July 1986. Forensic similarities linked Dawn's killing to the unsolved murder of fifteen-year-old Lynda Mann almost three years earlier, on 21 November 1983; both girls had attended Lutterworth Grammar School, both had been brutally raped, and both murders took place within a mile of each other. DNA evidence established that the same man had committed both crimes, but when Jeffreys compared the evidence with Buckland's DNA, his conclusions were startling – Buckland had not killed either girl. His confession had been completely fabricated, and he was released having already served three months in prison. Coincidentally, he was cleared on the third anniversary of Lynda Mann's murder. The real culprit was established by DNA two years later. *(See 1988.)*

☆ FIRST conviction secured through DNA evidence

Robert Melias, Bristol. Friday 13 November 1987

In January 1987 Mclias, heavy-drinking labourer, raped a 45-year-old disabled woman in her own house in Avonmouth, Bristol, then robbed her of jewellery. The woman picked him out in an identity parade, as a result of which his DNA was compared with that from semen stains on her clothing and found to be a perfect match. Melias maintained that he was innocent until two days before his trail was due to start, changing his plea when scientists stated that the chance of a false match was one in four million. He was sentenced to eight years for the rape and five for the robbery.

☆ FIRST murder conviction on DNA evidence

Colin Pitchfork, Leicester. Friday 22 January 1988

In 1987, after DNA had cleared Richard Buckland of raping and murdering two Leicestershire schoolgirls *(see above)*, police decided to take blood and saliva for DNA testing from every local male between the ages of 17 and 34. Bakery worker Colin

Pitchfork, who had previous convictions for exposing himself, said that he feared the police might 'fit him up' and bullied co-worker Ian Kelly to act as a stand-in. Using a fake passport as proof of identity, Kelly took Pitchfork's blood test for him. On 1 August 1987, while drinking with three fellow employees, Kelly revealed what he had done and six weeks later, after wrestling with her conscience, one of the three colleagues told the police. Pitchfork, 27, was arrested on 19 September 1987 and became the 4,583rd male to be tested as part of the investigation. It proved his guilt and he was sentenced to life imprisonment. Pitchfork said that in both cases he only intended to expose himself (something he claimed to have done to a thousand women) but, realising that as locals they could identify him, he was forced into killing them.

☆ FIRST conviction of computer hacker

Donald Burleson, Fort Worth, Texas. Tuesday 20 September 1988

Burleson was the computer security director and computer operations manager of a Fort Worth life insurance agency and securities firm known as USPA & IRA. He was fighting to stop USPA & IRA withholding income tax from his pay, and on 18 September 1985 he was fired when his supervisor discovered that he was using a USPA & IRA computer to prepare his suit against the company. In revenge Burleson decided to use a 'logic bomb' or 'worm' to corrupt the company's data. Three nights later he let himself into the facility at 03:00 using duplicate keys, then used an unauthorised backdoor password to enter the computer system and propagate the virus, which was designed to erase portions of the company's mainframe and then repeat the process if a predetermined value was not reset in a specific location. Ironically it was Burleson who started the legal proceedings that led to his prosecution – not content with the damage he had caused, he sued USPA & IRA in a local small claims court for back pay, so USPA & IRA filed a counterclaim, suing Burleson for unauthorised entry and interfering with the computer system. On 4 July 1986, a jury found Burleson guilty and he was fined $11,226 but he appealed and made only one $100 payment on the fine. In September 1988 in the 'First Virus Trial' a Texas state court convicted Burleson of 'harmful access to a computer', sentenced him to seven years of probation, and forced him to pay USPA & IRA $11,800 (the earlier fine of $11,226 plus interest).

☆ FIRST murderer to appear in a television reconstruction of the murder

John Tanner, Oxford. Monday 29 April 1991

In August 1990 Rachel McLean, a nineteen-year-old student at St Hilda's College, Oxford, began a stormy nine-month relationship with 22-year-old New Zealander John Tanner, a Nottingham University classics student. Tanner's behaviour became 'obsessive', culminating in a confrontation in April 1991 when McLean revealed she had been unfaithful and said that she wanted to end the relationship. A friend saw McLean saying farewell to Tanner at Oxford railway station but Tanner secretly returned to Oxford, strangled Rachel and hid her body under the floorboards of the house she shared with three other students. Police investigating Rachel's disappearance adopted an unusual investigation practice, making Tanner feel above suspicion by assigning two officers to become his new best friends. Newspapers had already hinted that Tanner might be involved in Rachel's disappearance and police used media attention to put pressure on him, convincing him to give a press conference. Tanner obliged, emotionally pleading for information and appealing for Rachel to get in touch. However, police had briefed reporters to ask the questions they couldn't, like 'did you kill Rachel?' Naturally he denied it, but a smirk before answering and lack of emotion convinced police he was their man. He also helped create an Identikit of a man with whom, he claimed, she had walked away from the station. Next, on 29 April, a reconstruction of the station farewell was broadcast on television, during which Tanner cuddled a policewoman wearing a wig and pretending to be Rachel. With the transmission Tanner's lies began to unravel as witnesses appeared who contradicted him. Police were convinced Rachel was dead, but had no corpse. They examined plans of the house where she lived, which revealed an air space under the floor and on 2 May they discovered her body. Tanner was arrested and confessed immediately, saying he had flown into a rage when Rachel had confessed her infidelity. At his trial at Birmingham Crown Court Tanner denied murder, pleading manslaughter on the grounds of provocation. He was released from prison after serving twelve years of a life sentence and returned to New Zealand.

☆ FIRST murder to be broadcast on British television

Albert Dryden, Eliza Lane, Butsfield, Consett, County Durham. Thursday 20 June 1991

Eccentric former steelworker Dryden built a 'hole-in-the-ground' bungalow for his mother without planning permission, claiming that permission was not required as only the roof was visible. As the eighteen month dispute with Derwentside Council dragged on Dryden became more bitter, threatening to pack one of his American cars with explosives and drive it into the council offices, and assaulting the council enforcement officer when he and Chief Planning Officer Harry Collinson tried to serve a summons on him. Collinson decided to personally supervise the demolition and invited the media to attend, assuming that should there be trouble their presence would contain any violence. On 20 June Collinson and Dryden stood talking over the gate at the entrance to Dryden's smallholding, with a TV crew and reporters looking on. Dryden disappeared into his caravan for a few minutes before emerging with a large gun in a holster. He walked to the fence, drew the revolver and pointed it at Collinson, who calmly asked the BBC cameraman to 'get a shot of the gun'. Dryden fired, hitting Collinson twice in the chest and then once in the head while he lay on the ground. Dryden then started shooting at council solicitor Michael Dunstan – Dunstan escaped unhurt but BBC reporter Tony Belmont was hit in the arm and PC Stephen Campbell was shot in the the buttock. The murder was transmitted on televisions around the world and Dryden was subsequently jailed for life. When PC Campbell recovered from his buttock wound he had to be transferred from Consett to nearby Stanley because local schoolchildren would taunt him with shouts of 'two arseholes'.

❑ ONLY prosecution for molesting a dolphin

Alan Cooper, Newcastle upon Tyne. Friday 13 December 1991

When a twelve-foot bottle-nose dolphin swam into Amble Harbour, Northumberland, 38-year-old animal rights campaigner Alan Cooper was delighted to be able to swim with it. He was less delighted to find himself in court accused of 'outraging public decency' by 'committing a lewd, obscene, and disgusting act' on the dolphin. Witnesses claimed that Cooper had 'masturbated the half-ton mammal as it floated on its back' and one of them, Fiona Huntingdon of International Dolphin Watch, said she was 'absolutely shocked and horrified'. Dolphin trainer William Prickett stated that when a swimmer was hooked by a dolphin's penis 'all the dolphin is trying to do is find a grip to get its jollies' but other expert witnesses testified that male dolphins use their erections not just sexually but socially as well, stating that the dolphin was using his penis as a 'finger of friendship' and that no sexual inference should be drawn. Cooper defended his actions by saying 'A male dolphin uses its penis in an entirely non-sexual way as a means of exploring things and pulling swimmers along'. On 13 December 1991, at the end of a five day trial, Cooper was cleared of sexually molesting Freddie the Dolphin. Summing up, the Judge said of the £337,500 trial that it had been the most expensive lesson in dolphin sociology that he had ever heard of. The press dubbed the whole case 'Flipping Crazy'.

❑ ONLY Amish convicted of homicide

Edward Gingerich, Mill Village, Pennsylvania. Thursday 18 March 1993

The Amish are a strict Anabaptist Christian denomination who aim to preserve the simple outlook of their forebears, but at dusk on 18 March 1993 Amish lumber-mill operator Edward Gingerich, 28, behaved in a far from Christian manner. In front of two of their children he attacked his wife Katie in the kitchen of their farmhouse, knocking her over and stomping on her face violently enough to crush her skull. He then tore off her clothing, grabbed a steak knife and began a Jack-the-Ripper-like frenzy, slashing open her belly and removing her heart, lungs, spleen, liver, kidneys, ovaries and intestines, which he stacked in a neat pile beside her corpse. After washing himself in the sink he threw his Bible into the fireplace, and told the children to put on their coats on, saying: 'I'm taking you to Granddad's, then I'm coming back to burn down the house.' Convicted of involuntary manslaughter, Gingerich was sentenced to imprisonment at the State Correctional Institution in Pittsburgh for a minimum term of two and a half and a maximum of five years.

☆ FIRST execution of a criminal convicted on DNA evidence

☆ FIRST US doctor to refuse to participate in an execution after an AMA ruling

Timothy W Spencer, Greensville Correctional Center, Greensville, Virginia. 23:13 Wednesday 27 April 1994

Spencer, known as 'The Southside Strangler', raped and strangled four women during an eleven week period in 1987, attacking his victims as they slept in their own homes. Debbie Dudley Davis, 35, was found naked on the bed of her apartment; neuro-surgeon Dr Susan Elizabeth Hellams, 32, was found gagged, raped and strangled in her bedroom wardrobe; student Diane Cho, 15, was raped and strangled while her parents and brother slept in the same apartment; and Susan Tucker, 44, was raped and murdered in her apartment. Spencer had bound the hands of three of the four women to a neck ligature, so that the more they struggled the more they choked. All four were killed while Spencer was signed out on weekend release from a Richmond halfway house, having being released from a state prison where he had served three years of a ten-year sentence for burglary. No victim survived to identify him, no fingerprints were found and no one confessed, but DNA tests confirmed that sperm traces found at the crime scene belonged to Spencer. After his conviction, Spencer refused to speak to criminal profilers seeking to analyse his behaviour and motives. When warden Ellis B Wright Jr asked Spencer if he had last words Spencer said, 'Yeah, I think.' Then he fell silent and looked around. After about twenty seconds he nodded, and the leather death mask was strapped on. His fists clenched when he received the first of four jolts in the oak electric chair. Outside the prison death-penalty opponents sang

'Amazing Grace', while high school students yelled, 'Kill the bitch.' Spencer's milestone conviction prompted Virginia to open the first state DNA laboratory in the USA and apparently inspired mystery writer Patricia D Cornwell's 1990 novel *Postmortem*. It is a legal requirement that a doctor be present at executions to supply a death certificate and, in the event the condemned is still alive, to recommend a more effective measure to kill him. Such laws place doctors in a dilemma, especially with the electric chair, where the condemned may be subjected to prolonged agony of up to thirty minutes. A ruling by the American Medical Association (AMA) suggests that a doctor's participation in an execution constitutes a violation of medical ethics, and on that basis Dr. Balvir Kapil, chief physician at the Department of Corrections in Richmond, Virginia, refused to attend Spencer's execution, thus becoming the first doctor to act on this ruling. In his absence a private practitioner, Dr Alvin Harris, filled in the death certificate, arguing that the AMA ruling was in conflict with state law. As a result of his ethical refusal Dr. Kapil was transferred to another department.

☆ FIRST man convicted for attempting to rape a man

Andrew Richards, Old Bailey, London. Friday 9 June 1995

Richards, a multiple sex attacker from Neath in West Glamorgan, Wales, was jailed for life at the Old Bailey for attempting to rape a man. The Criminal Justice Act of 1994 made male-rape an offence – previously the charge would have been buggery, carrying a maximum ten-year sentence, while rape or attempted rape carries a maximum of life. On 11 May, 26-year-old Richards had attacked and attempted to rape an unnamed 18-year-old male. Psychiatric reports concluded that he suffered a psychopathic personality disorder compounded by excessive use of glue, alcohol and drugs.

* LAST legal hanging in the USA

William Bailey, Delaware Correctional Center, Smyrna, Delaware. 00:04 Thursday 25 January 1996

In 1980 Bailey, an incorrigible thief and the nineteenth of 23 children, escaped from prison and robbed a liquor store before going to a farm belonging to 79-year-old Gilbert Lamberston and his wife Clara, 72. There, intent on stealing their pickup truck, he shot them, arranged their bodies in chairs and fled on foot to nearby woods where he was captured by a state trooper. Asked why he committed the murders, Bailey said: 'I don't really know. I just know that I feel bad about it. It hurts sometimes when I think about it. When I say hurt, I think about the Lambertsons and how much they hate me and I start to cry and sometimes I cry myself to sleep at night.' He said he did not remember the killings because he was drunk and high on Valium at the time. Bailey spent his last 24 hours in a caravan next to the outdoor gallows. His last meal was a well-done steak, a baked potato with sour cream and butter, buttered rolls, peas and vanilla ice cream. Just before midnight he was led into the yard which was surrounded by prison guards with dogs. Two guards, wearing black jumpsuits and black hoods held in place by baseball caps, escorted Bailey up the 23 steps to the gallows platform 15 feet above the ground, where official hangman Warden Robert Snyder was waiting. Asked if he had any last words Bailey said, 'No sir.' At 00:04 Snyder pulled the lever with both hands – Bailey dropped ten feet and his body spun six times anti-clockwise, and eleven minutes later the doctor pronounced him dead. One of the victim's two sons, 68-year-old Saxton Lambertson, witnessed the execution along with seven reporters and twelve official witnesses. He said his parents 'were very innocent people. They were old and small and he was a big brute. He chose to shoot them so he chose to die.'

* LAST execution by firing squad in the US

John Albert Taylor, Utah. 00:03 Friday 26 January 1996

Taylor was executed for the 1988 rape and murder of eleven-year-old Charla King, who was found in her family's Texas apartment strangled with a telephone cord and gagged with a pair of panties. Taylor chose the firing squad as his method of execution to the dismay of state politicians, who were afraid of negative publicity because Utah had applied for the Winter Olympics in 2002. However, Taylor insisted because he wanted to make the killing awkward for the state, and said he did not want to flop around 'like a dying fish' from a lethal injection. More than 150 television crews from around the world came to record his execution, with nine media witnesses allowed to record the actual event. Taylor was brought to the execution room dressed in dark clothing – so that the blood wouldn't show – and positioned in a mesh chair with channels on the sides and a pan underneath to collect the blood and bodily fluids that would be spilled. A doctor located his heart then a white circle was affixed over the spot with Velcro and Taylor was restrained in the chair by his arms, legs, chest and head. Behind the chair were thick sandbags to absorb the bullets and prevent them from ricocheting around the room. Five gunports faced him 23 feet away, one for each of five gunmen – including the detective who had investigated the case, who had volunteered for the firing squad. One of the five bullets loaded into the .30 calibre rifles was a blank, so that none of the gunmen knew if s/he was responsible for Taylor's death. Warden Hank Galetka covered Taylor's head with a thick, black hood, and at 00:03 Galetka counted to three and the gunmen fired. As the volley struck Taylor's hands squeezed up, went down, and came up and squeezed again. His chest was covered with blood. Four minutes later, a doctor pronounced him dead.

☆ FIRST Briton to be executed in Singapore

John Martin Scripps, Changi Prison. 06:37 Friday 19 April 1996

Scripps was a long-term criminal who graduated from London burglar to drug smuggler and then serial killer, using the butchery skills he had learned in prison to dismember his victims. Two of Scripps' relatives served life prison sentences for murder in England but he was not so lucky. His execution was a fight to the death: it took twelve guards twenty minutes to force him into the holding cell adjacent to the gallows, during which he sustained multiple bruising, two black eyes and a broken nose, jaw and cheekbone; on the scaffold he lost all control of his bodily functions; and then, Scripps having refused to be weighed (which meant that the hangman could not properly set the length of the rope) the misjudged drop caused his head to be almost ripped from his body.

☆ FIRST virtual-reality reconstruction of a crime scene to be used in court evidence

Senior Sgt Adrian Freeman and Sgt Troy O'Malley, Queensland Supreme Court, Cairns, Australia. Monday 14 September 1998

Michiko Okuyama, a 22-year-old Japanese tourist, disappeared on 20 September 1997 during a shopping trip in the centre of Cairns. It was later found that a sixteen-year-old boy (unnamed for legal reasons) lured her into an abandoned warehouse where, in a sound-proof steel vault, he battered her so severely that she drowned in her own blood. He then put the naked corpse into a rubbish bin and wheeled it five kilometres through the city streets before dumping it in a nearby swamp, where it was found on 6 October after a massive police search. At the trial Freeman presented a dozen digital photographs of the crime scene and then, using software developed by him and O'Malley, formerly a technician in commercial television, he 'stitched' together interactive 360-degree views, allowing the jury to 'walk' through the crime scene. Freeman, who presented his evidence over two days, said later, 'It was a complicated case in relation to the layout of the warehouse where the girl was murdered. Virtual reality was used to show the jury the layout, and also in reference to a number of incidents that occurred in the warehouse during that time.' On 23 September the boy was found guilty and sentenced to life imprisonment. After the trial the judge, Justice Stan Jones, described the application of VR technology as 'excellent', adding, 'Crimes are committed in environments that can change quite dramatically in the time it takes to get a case to trial. The advantage [of this technology] is that you have a crime scene presented in a way in which you can take the witnesses through it, and move around. "I came through this door and saw this" is a great deal better than having a jury try to remember photographs.'

☆ FIRST British professional footballer to play in a league match wearing an electronic tag

Gary Croft, Portman Road, Ipswich. 16:26 Saturday 15 January 2000

On Monday 10 January 2000 Croft was released and tagged after serving about a month of a four-month sentence for driving while disqualified and perverting the course of justice. The following Saturday the 25-year-old Ipswich Town player was named as a substitute for the First Division match against Swindon Town at Ipswich's Portman Road ground, and in the 71st minute he replaced Mike Stockwell on the wing, the electronic tag clearly visible on his left ankle. Ipswich won the game 3-0. Under the terms of his release Croft had to wear the device for the next three weeks, obeying a night-time curfew from 19:00 until 07:00. It should be noted that Croft played for Ipswich Town Reserves wearing his tag in their 1-0 win over Gillingham the previous Wednesday afternoon, but that was not a full league match.

DID YOU KNOW?

Gary Croft (*above*) made his England under-21s debut against Brazil under-21s on 6 June 1995 – the same match in which a certain David Beckham made his debut.

☆ FIRST parent jailed for allowing children to play truant

Patricia Amos, Banbury Magistrates' Court, Oxfordshire. Thursday 9 May 2002

After two years of legal wrangling, Amos was sentenced to 60 days' imprisonment for not regularly sending her two daughters to secondary school – a new deterrent for errant parents who could previously have expected a hefty fine. It is estimated that five million school days are lost each year to truancy and absences.

☆ FIRST posthumous pardon in the legal history of New York State

Lenny Bruce, New York. Tuesday 23 December 2003

In response to a petition prepared by Robert Corn-Revere and filed by Ron Collins and David Skover, Lenny Bruce was posthumously pardoned by New York Republican Governor George Pataki for the obscenity conviction arising from his 1964 performances in New York's Cafe Au Go Go. Pataki called his decision 'a declaration of New York's commitment to upholding the First Amendment'.

☆ FIRST conviction using DNA 'familial searching'

Craig Harman, Old Bailey, London. Monday 19 April 2004

Harman, twenty, admitted killing 53-year-old lorry driver Michael Little on 1 March 2003 but only conceded his guilt after being confronted with DNA evidence six months later. While drunk Harman, then a teenage sports-shop assistant, hurled a brick from a footbridge over the M3 near Camberley, Surrey, which crashed through the windscreen of Little's lorry, hitting him in the chest and causing fatal heart injuries. The brick was found in the cab and bore traces of Harman's blood from an earlier hand injury caused by breaking into a car. The blood didn't match anything on the national DNA database (the largest in the world with around 2.35 million samples) because Harman had no previous convictions. However, using 'familial searching', which is based on the fact that people who are related have similar DNA profiles, police matched the blood on the brick by sixteen points out of twenty to a close relative who was on the database. As a result Harman was sentenced to six years for manslaughter.

☆ FIRST ASBO (Anti-Social Behaviour Order) to be issued in the UK

Thomas Harcombe, Somerset, England. Friday 17 September 2004

Harcombe was arrested on 2 August for exposing himself in Taunton Deane town centre. Taunton Deane Magistrates Court subsequently issued the 38-year-old with an Anti-Social Behaviour Order prohibiting him from loitering within 50 metres of any school in England or Wales with pupils under the age of 15. (*See also 30 January 1907*)

☆ FIRST internet murder

Rachelle Waterman, Craig, Alaska. Sunday 14 November 2004

Shortly after midnight on 14 November 2004, sixteen-year-old Rachelle Waterman (aka smchyrocky) allegedly recruited her former sexual partners Brian Radel and Jason Arrant (both 24) to bludgeon to death her 48-year-old mother, Lauri Waterman. Later that day a local hunter discovered Lauri's body and her burnt-out van on a remote logging road, something of which Rachelle casually informed the world via her internet live-journal: four days after the murder she posted the message: 'Just to let everyone know, my mother was murdered. I won't have computer acess [sic] until the weekend or so because the police took my computer to go through the hard drive. I thank everyone for their thoughts and e-mails, I hope to talk to you when I get my computer back.' The following day she was arrested. Subsequently more than 7,000 comments were posted on the journal, transforming the case into an internet phenomenon, with Rachelle dubbed the LiveJournal murderer. Arrant and Radel pleaded guilty to first degree murder in June 2005 and testified against Waterman as part of their plea bargain. She was charged with first degree murder but her trial resulted in a hung jury, 10-2 in favour of acquittal. A mistrial was declared, and on 7 March 2006, Judge Collins dismissed all charges against Waterman, ruling that her videotaped testimony from the day of her arrest (the main reason for her indictment) was coerced. Lack of motive proved a problem for prosecutors, although in her online journal Waterman often mentioned arguments with her mother, and on 16 April she had posted the message: 'I had a bad night and a bad day. This is my warning to all of you: if you piss me off you die.' If she is ever found guilty she will be the blogging world's first killer.

☆ FIRST airline pilot jailed under new alcohol legislation

Heikki Tallila, Manchester Crown Court. Thursday 2 December 2004

Under a new law making it legal for police to breath test air crew Tallila was arrested on 23 August 2004 just minutes before he was due to take off from Manchester Airport in a Finnair Boeing 757 bound for Turkey with 225 passengers. A blood test revealed that he had 49mg of alcohol per 100ml of blood – more than twice the legal limit of 20mg. He was jailed for six months.

☆ FIRST woman convicted of using Rohypnol

Selina Hakki, Middlesex Guildhall Crown Court. Monday 17 January 2005

Hakki, a 37-year-old Guyana-born mother-of-two was sentenced to five years for drugging and robbing a film director and a banker, and police stated that forensic evidence linked her to six similar crimes whose victims were too embarrassed to press charges. She was convicted on two charges of administering a stupefying drug ('date rape' drug Rohypnol) and two of theft. One of the victims, Volker Volger, a banker who had been celebrating his 36th birthday in the rooftop bar of the Hilton Hotel, was asked whether he went home with Volker and had sex. He replied, 'Unfortunately I did not.'

☆ FIRST criminal sentenced by telephone

Aftab Ahmed, Ipswich Crown Court. Wednesday 2 February 2005

Ahmed, a 44-year-old taxi driver from Bury St Edmunds, telephoned Ipswich Crown Court to say he would be late for his hearing because he was stuck in traffic behind a fatal car crash.

Judge Caroline Ludlow telephoned back and told Ahmed not to interrupt while she sentenced him. For failing to disclose information when he was made bankrupt, Judge Ludlow sentenced Ahmed to do 140 hours community service and pay £750 costs. When asked if he had anything to say he complained about the costs.

☆ FIRST killing by a Sky Marshal

Rigoberto Alpizar, Miami International Airport. 14:00 Wednesday 7 December 2005

Alpizar, 44, was gunned down after boarding an Orlando-bound flight and running down the aisle shouting that he had a bomb. Terrified passengers watched as undercover Sky Marshals, introduced in the wake of the 9/11 attacks, pursued Alpizar out of the aircraft door and onto the gangway where, after twice refusing instructions to lie on the ground, he reached into his bag – Sky Marshals then shot him four or five times. Federal sources later disclosed that Alpizar had not been carrying a bomb or weapon.

☆ FIRST conviction based on evidence from a camera fitted to a policeman's hat

Fiona Linehan, Plymouth Magistrates' Court, Devon. Wednesday 22 March 2006

Charged with assaulting a police officer, 22-year-old Linehan was advised to plead guilty by her defence lawyer, who had seen footage from the helmet camera of Linehan shouting and spitting at Sergeant Olly Taylor in the back of a police car. As well as four counts of assaulting Taylor, Linehan also admitted two counts of assaulting her boyfriend, and was given a supervision order by magistrates.

DEDICATIONS & ACKNOWLEDGEMENTS

For Wilf Gregg, who not only built the finest true crime reference library in Britain but is also a kind, generous and wise benefactor to all crime historians – especially ones who can't find what they are looking for!

With thanks to:

Sue Beadle
David & Maureen Chambers
Malcolm Croft
Richard Crowest
Paul Donnelley
Phil & Mary Harrison
Roddy Langley
Norman Lawrence
Loretta Lay (www.laybooks.com)
Kevin Major-Morrell
Matthew Spicer
Linda Yaffe

Jeremy Beadle is best known as a highly successful television presenter and programme maker. He is equally at home as an oddity hunter. His 25,000 volume library is dominated by true crime books. He won both Celebrity Mastermind – specialist subject 'London Murder 1900-1940' – and Discovery Channel's 'The Trial of Jack the Ripper'. He has hosted many Jack the Ripper conferences and once shared a flat with a friend who later spent twenty years in a Greek Prison for murder.

Ian Harrison has written more than twenty books on subjects ranging from ancient battlefields to modern airports. He worked as a researcher for television documentaries and then crossed over to publishing after co-writing Prince Edward's *Crown and Country* from the television series of the same name. Ian's titles include *Where Were You When......?* (Collins & Brown) and the hugely popular '*Book of......*' series: *The Book of Firsts*, *The Book of Inventions, The Book of Lasts* and *The Book of Duos*, which between them have been translated into sixteen languages. He was born in Castleford and now lives in London with his wife and two daughters.